PLACE THAT PLANT

PLACE
THAT
PLANT

Frances Welland

This is a Parragon Book
This edition published in 2003

Parragon
Queen Street House
4 Queen Street
Bath BA1 1HE, UK

Conceived, edited, illustrated
and produced by Robert Ditchfield Publishers

ISBN 1-40540-433-7

A copy of the British Library Cataloguing in Publication
Data is available from the Library.

Typeset by Action Publishing Technology Ltd, Gloucester
Colour origination by Colour Quest Graphic Services Ltd.
London E9
Printed and bound in China

Half Title: This elegant assembly of plants makes a perfect
picture. The formal ornament is surrounded by plants of
relaxed shape yet it is buttressed behind and on either side
by the clipped hedge and twin box pyramids.

Frontispiece: A clever composition in misty colours for autumn.
Michaelmas daisies surf forwards at the front of a border.
Their flat rayed flowers make a contrast in shape to the
poker heads of red persicaria and white cimicifuga in the
background.

THE PURPOSE of this book is to act as an illustrated guide to putting the right plants in the right positions. Its intention is to simplify that most difficult part of garden-making which consists of choosing appropriate plants and planning their combinations.

Ranges of plants are presented in groups according to their attributes and their suitability for a particular setting or soil. Some interrelation is inevitable, and certain key plants may crop up in two or even three sections, as there are many subjects that can be put to multiple use: for example, to embossing a paved terrace or, alternatively, to forming a carpet at the foot of a hedge.

Nearly 800 plants have been illustrated here. The choice is based on many factors. Floral beauty, perfume, grace of leaf, trunk and habit, distinction, suitability for a particular purpose, ease of temperament, all these factors play their part singly or in combination.

INFORMATION GIVEN IN THIS BOOK

Where appropriate, approximate measurements of a plant's height have been given, and also the spread where this is significant, in both metric and imperial measures. The height is the first measurement, as for example 1.2m × 60cm/ 4 × 2ft. However, both height and spread vary so greatly from garden to garden since they depend on soil, climate and position, that these measurements are offered as guides only. This is especially true of trees and shrubs where ultimate growth can be unpredictable.

The following symbols are also used:
E   = evergreen
○   = thrives best or only in full sun
◐   = thrives best or only in part-shade
●   = succeeds in full shade
LH = will not tolerate or thrive in a chalky or limy earth and prefers or must have acid, peaty soil to succeed.

Where no sun symbol and no reference to sun or shade is made in the text, it can be assumed that the plant tolerates sun or light shade.

Fully hardy: means that the plant can survive winters in temperate regions.

Not fully hardy: means that it is probable that the plant will need shelter and protection during winter in temperate regions.

Tender: means that even in mild winter areas the plant may need protection to survive or can be grown under glass.

PLANT NAMES

For ease of reference this book gives the botanical name under which a plant is most widely listed for the gardener. These names are sometimes changed and in such cases the new name has been included. Common names are given wherever they are in frequent use.

POISONOUS PLANTS

In recent years, concern has been voiced about poisonous plants or plants which can cause allergic reactions if touched. The fact is that many plants are poisonous, some in a particular part, others in all their parts. For the sake of safety, it is always, without exception, essential to assume that no part of a plant should be eaten unless it is known, without any doubt whatsoever, that the plant or its part is edible and that it cannot provoke an allergic reaction in the individual person who samples it. It must also be remembered that some plants can cause severe dermatitis, blistering or an allergic reaction if touched, in some individuals and not in others. It is the responsibility of the individual to take all the above into account.

WATER IN THE GARDEN

All water gardens are beautiful, but sadly they can be dangerous, mostly to children who can drown in even a few inches of water, or sometimes to adults. We would urge readers where necessary to take account of this and provide a reliable means of protection if they include water in the garden.

Contents

A white haze of *Crambe cordifolia* hangs over purple geranium and *Stachys macrantha* 'Robusta'.

Brilliant blue and gold from a partnership of delphinium and *Gentiana lutea* backed by a Japanese maple (*Acer shirasawanum* 'Aureum').

HOW TO PLACE PLANTS

The challenge that people face when planning their gardens is where and how to place plants that will achieve the effects they desire. In most cases plants will be assembled in beds or borders and the scope for planning these is almost limitless. In theory they can be any shape or size, irregular or formal, anchored to a wall or forming islands. They can be made on the level, sunken or raised. They can be designed as specialist growing areas with imported soil – peat beds, for example, containing lime-intolerant plants in an alkaline garden. They might not look like beds at all but bear a camouflaging top layer of gravel or chippings.

As for the plants, the permutations are even greater. Even in a tiny garden, a mixed border can contain alpines, bulbs, hardy herbaceous plants, tender annuals, biennials, shrubs and, quite possibly, a tree or two. Vegetables and herbs may prove to be necessary additions.

Indeed, the term 'beds and borders' covers so many variables of shape, size and plant life, that it is easy to lose sight of the main common denominator. Beds and borders are collections of plants. To be successful, they must make a collective impact and form pictures.

This is the overriding principle when composing any bed or border, whatever its dimensions and whatever its style. If the border looks as if it is simply a number of individual plants which happen to be growing in the same area of earth, it is a failure.

Other rules of design are rather more flexible and depend on the situation of the beds, on the space at your disposal and, not least, on the amount of time you are able and/or willing to spend on maintenance.

To plan a border, you therefore have to take yourself into account (whether you will weed and water as required) as well as the options your garden offers in terms of soil, space and aspect.

SITE

Small beds can be tucked into almost any space providing the soil is suitable, and light, air and moisture are sufficient for good plant growth. Large mixed borders, however, are another matter. The limitations of a garden may be such that only one area is remotely suitable for a border. Nevertheless, if a choice is possible, it helps to bear in mind the following factors. First, that a site open to the sun permits you to grow the greatest range of plants. Second, a big, deep border is far superior to one of ribbon width; 1.8m/6ft is minimum depth for less substantial plants, 3m/10ft more suitable if large shrubs are to be included. Third, a wall, fence, hedge or house-backed border will provide a frame for the picture, an advantage missing in island beds which lack any such anchorage. On the other hand, island sites do give scope for beds which can be viewed from all sides (a point to be taken into account when planning their design). They also have the practical asset of reducing the need for staking, as the stems of plants are less drawn in a bed where light reaches all parts.

DESIGN

It is best to work out the scheme on graph paper first. It will still be hard to visualize this flat plan, so you can either try a sketch or draw the plants onto a photograph of the site.

The airy verticals of verbascum and clary give a relaxed impressionistic effect that belies careful planning.

Foxglove, euphorbia and allium are grouped to form a harmonious colour combination and a wonderful contrast in texture.

However, even this preliminary stage is impossible unless you know your plants. And this means knowing not only the colour of their flowers, but their season of bloom, their foliage, the plants' height, habit of growth and preference for soil and aspect. Given this grasp of the individual, you can then plan the whole.

In the pages that follow, plants are suggested which can be grouped in categories which are useful to consider when assembling a border (such as foliage plants, edge-breakers, winter flowers etc.)

When you plan, you have to visualize not only details like the neighbouring value of two or three plants in terms of their colour and season, but also principles such as how long you want your border to remain in leaf and colour. If it is in permanent view from the house, the answer is probably throughout the year. In this case, refer also to Evergreens on pages 46–51.

The most impressive borders are always designed not just as colour set pieces but to ensure contrast of form and equally of leaf texture. Lacy foliage appears more delicate and refined against plants with entire, leathery leaves. A mass of flowery spires will be stabilized by neighbouring hummocks.

Plant in bold groups for maximum effect.

This formal planting is a splendid example of the powerful effect that
can be achieved with a limited variety of plants and a restrained palette.

Generosity of treatment is vital and five of one kind of herbaceous plant in any one spot is not too many, unless the plant is very substantial or the bed unusually small. Such groups, particularly when they have a bold identity and shape, can be repeated at intervals across a border to give a dominant theme in any one season, other plants succeeding in prominence as the season wears on and changing the theme.

Fronts of beds and borders are usually filled with prostrate or low plants, but it is more arresting to allow an occasional tall and clumping plant to infiltrate these ranks. Organized variety is the ideal, not monotonous predictability.

Spacing between groups is rather more a question of experience, but certainly allow some room over and above your spacing of the individual plants. Allow, also, regular spaces for stepping-stones, so that you can enter the bed.

Easy maintenance will depend on the amount of shrubs you can include, and also labour-saving perennials (pages 160–5) which need neither staking nor regular division and lifting. Ground-cover plants (pages 104–9) will be of some use here, too, but with the qualification that their vigour may involve you in having to control their tendency to roam.

Where plants spill over the edge onto

grass and where the setting is suitably formal, it will ease the mower's lot if a line of paving is laid beside the bed, slightly below the level of the lawn.

TREE AND SHRUB BORDERS

A border that is composed mainly of trees and large shrubs requires a slightly different approach, for very large subjects are obviously substantial enough not to need grouping. (Smaller shrubs, however, may still require to be planted in masses, if their presence is to be noticed.)

Good design in this kind of border depends greatly on form. Colour is usually a secondary factor. It is always a good plan, however, to include deliberately, some late-flowering shrubs for colour (buddlejas, hebes, eucryphia, hydrangeas, selected roses, caryopteris, perovskia and a further selection on pages 120–7), as most shrubs flower earlier in the season. Autumn colouring or berrying trees and shrubs can also look wonderfully rich at a time when the other inmates are dull or decayed. The ideal is to keep a border in a state of continuous development; fading areas have to be replaced by blossoming, expanding plants, if it is not to become drab, and, being large, dominating the whole garden by its dowdiness.

TERRACES AND PATIOS

A terrace or a patio is the sole architectural feature which is essential in most gardens. It has a utilitarian function: to allow the owner to sit, eat and entertain in an area which is adjacent and convenient to the house. Yet, in a large garden, it has an aesthetic and ideal function too, which is to ease the house in stages into the garden beyond, a purpose it fulfils by combining masonry and plants.

Here more than elsewhere, masonry has the upper hand over plants. It is not a place

for confusion and plants cannot enjoy the relatively unfettered freedom that may be theirs in wilder or more spacious parts of the garden. Nonetheless they are essential and usually under-used ingredients which will soften and decorate the harsh architectural contours and bring movement and change to the static surface.

It is easier to plan if you visualize it as an area with a clear centre, spacious enough to allow room for your activities or relaxation and for features such as a specimen tree for shade or a small formal pool. Plants can surf forwards luxuriantly over the edges of this area, some rocketing upwards to give vertical contrast to the horizontal lines, others (outside the main traffic lines) encrusting the surface and even encroaching abundantly so long as this does not cause complications. Potted plants can be placed where they cannot grow in the earth and positioned to give a visual balance to other areas.

Remember too that on a drowsy afternoon or at the stillness of dusk, it is the scented flowers that will give you so much pleasure here.

ASSESSING AND PREPARING SOIL

Soil is either acid, neutral or alkaline, expressed in what is called the pH scale. Its acidity or alkalinity matters because lime-intolerant plants (such as rhododendrons, some heaths, camellias, etc.) will not thrive in an alkaline soil. You can buy soil-testing kits which will assess your soil type.

In other respects, certain soil-types are recognizable by their textures and should be treated accordingly. 1) Sandy soil is light, gritty and dries out quickly. Add peat or compost to improve its ability to hold moisture. 2) Chalky soil is shallow and sometimes has lumps of chalk or limestone in its subsoil. Add compost or rotted manure and

A Japanese maple is positioned against conifers for maximum effect when its foliage reddens in autumn.

PLANTING

The planting season for bare-rooted deciduous trees and shrubs is from late autumn to spring, but if the soil is frozen, very sticky or sodden when the plants arrive, make an earth trench in some spare ground and 'heel in' the plants until conditions improve. Evergreens are better planted in either early autumn or mid-spring when the soil is warmer. Container-grown plants can be planted at any time of the year. Soak the root ball well before removing the polythene and planting. All new plants must be watered regularly during dry spells for up to a year after planting.

Where each tree, shrub or plant will grow, prepare a flat-bottomed hole deeper and wider than the roots will occupy. Put rotted manure or compost right at the base and cover with good topsoil (so that the roots cannot touch the manure). Place the plant in position, pouring damp peat or an equivalent mixed with a little fertilizer around the roots. Don't plant deeper than the soil mark on the stem (with the exception of clematis; see page 222). Firm the soil over the roots when they are covered and re-firm after a heavy frost. Secure planting is always essential.

Trees need a stake placed stoutly in position before the roots are inserted in the hole. Tie the stem to the stake with a soft rubber or cloth tie which will not chafe the bark.

Water all new plants well to settle in, and thereafter keep free of weeds. In dry weather or drying winds, young conifers may need their foliage regularly sprayed as well as their roots watered.

In all cases, a mulch will help to prevent the newly planted subjects from drying out before their roots can establish themselves. But if planting in the depth of winter when the soil is cold, wait until spring before

fertilizers. 3) Clay soil is heavy and sticky in winter like plasticine, yet dries out in summer to concrete. Dig it over roughly in the autumn to allow frosts to break it down and add strawy compost or organic matter. If the clay is very heavy, it is possible to add garden lime over dry soil. Don't add any fertilizers for at least one month before liming and for three months afterwards. Also, liming means you cannot grow lime-intolerant plants in the soil, nor even in those areas into which the soil or water might leach to any extent.

applying the material. Time it so that the soil is still moist but beginning to warm.

MAINTENANCE

A border either has to be under continuous cultivation so that it is kept clean and weed-free, or else you have to find some means of keeping the weeds down if not out. Ground-cover plants, whether shrubby or herbaceous, are one way of doing this. Mulching in spring is another. In this case, allow the soil to lose its winter chill; at that spring stage where it is slightly warmed yet still moist, put on it (around each plant) a thick quilt – from 2.5cm to 7.5cm/1 to 3in deep – of compost, pulverized tree bark, leaf-mould, peat or sawdust. This will also keep the soil moist for longer in the summer, reducing the need for watering. (Mulching is not, of course, used for gravel beds, where the actual chippings serve as a mulch.)

The advantage of leaf-mould, compost, pulverized tree bark and (if you can get it) straw with rotted farmyard manure is that these materials replace nutrients that have been used up by the plants or leached out of the soil. Otherwise, balanced artificial fertilizers can be used.

Staking is also a spring job, though (as a general rule) it is only necessary for plants which grow above 75cm–1m/2½–3ft. In exposed or windy positions, it may prove essential, however, for shorter plants. Brushwood, like pea-sticks, can be put around the plant so that the growing stems will be enclosed and supported by it in an unobtrusive manner. But delphiniums and other tall, very stout-stemmed flowers will have to be tied to stout stakes or canes.

Dead-heading in summer will not only keep a border looking trim, but will prolong the season by inducing the plant to produce further crops of flowers.

In autumn, the woody stems of hardy

Mauve-blue *Campanula lactiflora* (foreground) and *Salvia sclarea* var. *turkestanica* (background) with sulphur yellow sisyrinchium.

herbaceous plants should be cut back to the ground. But leave the stems on marginally tender plants, as they may be a small protection in severe winter snaps.

Before the onset of winter (certainly before the likelihood of any hard frost), all tender plants should have a protective covering of loosely packed bracken or grit or peat over the crowns. If they are tall plants, they ought to be wrapped up in a polythene or hessian blanket (ideally with loosely-packed dry straw within). If slugs are a pest, put grit round the crowns.

Plants for Specific Soils

Most plants are adaptable and will grow happily in a wide range of soils. Others, however, are fussier about the medium in which they are grown and some of these have very strict requirements indeed. If you test your soil, you will know whether it is heavy clay, alkaline or acid. This section of the book shows which plants will thrive in each of these situations.

Plants for Heavy Clay

Heavy clay soils are hard to work because they are waterlogged and sticky in winter, yet dry out in summer to resemble a form of concrete. Their other disadvantage is that they are slow to warm up in spring. However, they are fertile and will grow a wider range of plants if the structure can be lightened by the addition of compost or grit which will help to aerate the earth. Ideally this can be incorporated in the spring when the worst of the wet has drained. It is better to avoid working on the ground earlier in the year, because of the nature of the clay. At this time the heavy soil will become compacted if trodden on when sticky.
The following plants will tolerate heavy clay.

Abelia ○
All forms of this shrub need fertile soil but it must be well-drained. *A. schumannii* is valuable for its late flowering from summer to autumn. Needs shelter as not fully hardy. 1.5m/5ft H and W

Betula albo-sinensis. The white Chinese birch tree is noted for its fine rufous peeling bark, light green leaves and airy habit. 15 × 4.5m/49 × 15ft

Aesculus parviflora ○
The bottlebrush buckeye produces its candles of flowers from mid to late summer. It is also valuable for its changing leaf colour – from bronze when young, to green, to yellow in autumn. Shrubby growth of 3m/10ft H and W.

Betula ermanii
Another beautiful-barked birch, with a pinkish-cream trunk. Glossy leaves colour well in autumn. 15 × 4.5/49 × 15ft

Chaenomeles speciosa 'Nivalis'
Pretty form of 'japonica' with clusters of milky flowers over a long period in spring. 2.1m/7ft H and W

Cotinus coggygria (Smoke bush) ○
Bushy shrub noted for its masses of tiny flower stalks giving the effect of plumes of floss in later summer. Leaves turn red and gold in autumn. 5m/16ft H and W

Mahonia aquifolium E
The oregon grape is a tough spreading shrub with clustered yellow flowers in spring followed by bloomy purple-indigo berries. 1 × 1.5m/3 × 5ft

Rubus tricolor E: ◐●
Low arching shrub with glossy leaves and red bristly stems, and white flowers in midsummer. Useful for ground-cover. 60cm × 1.8m/2 × 6ft

Euonymus fortunei 'Silver Queen' E
Shrub which will also climb slowly against walls, with variegated leaves and insignificant tiny cream flowers in spring. 3 × 1.5m/10 × 5ft

Salix elaeagnos (syn. *rosmarinifolia*)
The hoary willow with elegant silver-green foliage. It grows fast to 3 × 4m/10 × 13ft, so be sure to allow it sufficient room.

17

Salix hastata 'Wehrhahnii'
Distinctive shrubby willow with dark purple stems studded with silver catkins in spring before the leaves develop. 1.2m/4ft H and W

Malus hupehensis (Hupeh crab)
Robust tree massed with large scented white flowers in mid to late spring, followed by small yellow crab apples in late summer and autumn. It makes a fine, decorative specimen tree. 7.5 × 6m/25 × 20ft

A SELECTION OF SHRUBS AND TREES THAT TOLERATE HEAVY CLAY

Acer platanoides 'Drummondii'
A. pseudoplatanus 'Brilliantissimum' p.236
Aesculus p.16
Alnus glutinosa p.221
Aralia elata p.92
Aucuba japonica p.196
Berberis p.63
Betula (Birch) (some varieties) p.16
Carpinus betulus p.200
Choisya ternata p.48
Corylus
Cotoneaster p.244
Crataegus (Hawthorn) p.200
Eucalyptus p.88
Fraxinus (Ash)
Hedera (Ivy) in variety
Kerria
Laburnum p.209
Magnolia × soulangeana p.237
Malus (Crab) p.244
Philadelphus p.181
Picea breweriana p.247
Platanus (Plane)
Populus (Poplar)
Potentilla p.146
Prunus (Cherry) in variety
Prunus laurocerasus p.198
Pyracantha p.198
Pyrus (Pear) p.73
Quercus (Oak) p.221
Ribes (Currant)
Rubus (Bramble)
Salix (Willow) in variety
Skimmia p.127
Sorbus p.73
Spiraea p.121
Symphoricarpus
Syringa (Lilac) p.181
Taxus (Yew) p.66
Tilia (Lime)
Viburnum p.77
Vinca p.111
Weigela p.93

Weigela florida **'Foliis
Purpureis'** ○
Bronze-purple leafed
shrub at its prettiest in late
spring/early summer with
its pink trumpet flowers.
1 × 1.5m/3 × 5ft

Prunus **'Kanzan'**
Familiar Japanese cherry tree with ascending habit in
youth, spreading in maturity. Prolific with its blossom
in spring. Needs good drainage. 10 × 7.5m/33 × 25ft

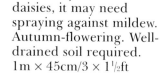

Aster novae-belgii 'Harrison's Blue' ○
Like many Michaelmas daisies, it may need spraying against mildew. Autumn-flowering. Well-drained soil required.
1m × 45cm/3 × 1¹⁄₂ft

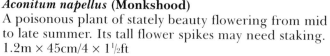

***Aconitum napellus* (Monkshood)**
A poisonous plant of stately beauty flowering from mid to late summer. Its tall flower spikes may need staking.
1.2m × 45cm/4 × 1¹⁄₂ft

Aster sedifolius (syn. *acris*)
A very floriferous and easy self-supporting bushy Michaelmas daisy. For well-drained soil. Its starry yellow-centred lavender-blue flowers are produced in autumn when they will make a great show.
75cm × 60cm/2¹⁄₂ × 2ft

Campanula latiloba
Easy, vigorous bellflower with leafy spikes of white, blue or amethyst flowers in summer. It will form dense mats and is suitable for sun or semi-shade. 60cm/2ft H and W

Doronicum cordatum (syn.
pardalianche) (**Leopard's
bane**)
Easy, cheerful spring-
flowering perennial which
forms a spreading clump.
75 × 60cm/2¹/₂ × 2ft

Eupatorium purpureum **(Joe Pye weed)** ◑
Very useful, if aggressive, perennial for its flowering in
late summer/early autumn. Its height makes it a strong
presence in the garden. 2.1 × 1m/7 × 3ft

Filipendula rubra
Stunning form of
meadowsweet with fluffy
flower plates in summer.
For moist sites. It is
another tall plant, which
flowers earlier than
Eupatorium and is less
coarse.

***Geranium himalayense* 'Gravetye'**
One of the many accommodating cranesbills, this plant
is summer-flowering and vigorous. Plan to include
several clumps when designing a summer bed.
45cm/1¹/₂ft H and W

Hemerocallis '**Summer Wine**'
Easy day lily with trumpet flowers produced over a long period in summer, though they are individually fleeting. 60cm/2ft H and W

Hosta undulata **var. undulata** ◐ ●
Variegated-leafed hosta with spikes of rich lilac flowers in summer. All hostas prefer moist soil. 45cm/1½ft H and W

Lamium maculatum '**Wootton Pink**' E: ◐
One of the 'dead-nettle' family. A pretty and tolerant groundcover plant with pink flowers over foliage which is striped white. It is best in semi-shade and prefers moist but well-drained soil. 15 × 30cm/6in × 1ft

Lysimachia clethroides ◑
Vigorous spreader with
crooks of white flowers in
late summer. Prefers moist
soil. 1m × 60cm/3 × 2ft

Lysimachia punctata
This somewhat coarse summer-flowering perennial
colonizes moist soil speedily. As the picture shows, it will
make a strong clump which may need controlling.
60cm/2 ft H and W

Petasites japonicus ◑ ●
Bizarre flowers in winter/early spring followed by large
umbrella leaves. Very invasive. Only for huge spaces
where it can be mown out as necessary. 1m/3ft ×
indefinite spread

Physalis alkekengi
(Chinese lantern)
Insignificant white flowers
are followed in autumn by
fruits covered with orange
calyces which give it its
common name. Invasive.
45 × 60cm/1½ × 2ft

Polemonium caeruleum **(Jacob's ladder)** ○
Orange-stamened, blue flower-cups in early summer
over ferny foliage. It will self-seed with some
enthusiam, but is easily weeded out.
60 × 45cm/2 × 1½ft

Solidago (**Golden rod**) ○
Perennial forming a clump with sprays of golden
flowerheads in later summer to autumn. Most species
are vigorous and will make a bold effect in the summer
border. Forms include 'Cloth of Gold' (45×60cm/1½×2ft)
and 'Golden Wings' (1.5×1m/5×3ft).

Telekia speciosa (syn.
Buphthalmum speciosum)
Vigorous summer-
flowering perennial with
large leaves and bold daisy
flowers. For moist soil.
1.2 × 1m/4 × 3ft

***Stachys macrantha* 'Robusta'**
Easy perennial flowering in midsummer over wrinkled
leaves. Good groundcover. It is shown here with the
creamy, feathery plumes of *Aruncus kneiffii*. 45cm/1½ft
H and W

Thalictrum aquilegiifolium
Slim stems support fluffy
white or mauve
flowerheads in early
summer above a mound of
elegant foliage.
1m × 45cm/3 × 1½ft

CONSIDER ALSO:

Ajuga p.104
Anemone × hybrida
  p.144
Alchemilla p.52
Astrantia p.161
Bergenia p.52
Brunnera p.92
Caltha p.182
Camassia p.132
Crocosmia masoniorum
Pachysandra
Polygonatum p.219
Pulmonaria p.137
Rudbeckia p.165
Saponaria p.97
Tellima p.105

Symphytum caucasicum
Easy, lusty comfrey which is coarse but useful in difficult
places. It is particularly well suited to the wilder parts of
the garden. 1.2m × 60cm/4 × 2ft

Plants for Alkaline Soils

Alkaline soil will grow a huge range of plants, though it will deny you the choice of almost all the ericaceous shrubs and trees, like rhododendrons, and a few other examples. It is usually hot, well-drained, and quick to dry out. Many perennials flourish in just these conditions, though larger plants may well require much more moisture than the soil will naturally retain. Incorporating plenty of humus will help water retention; and if this is done repeatedly, it may eventually also lower the degree of alkalinity.

Buddleja alternifolia ○
A butterfly bush, noted for its long strands of lilac flowers. It can be pruned into a small weeping 'tree' as shown. 3m/10ft H and W

Buddleja davidii 'Dartmoor' ○
This butterfly bush distinguishes itself by the presentation of its plumes of flowers in elegant arching groups. 2.11m/7ft H and W

Caragana arborescens 'Lorbergii'
Arching elegant shrub, sometimes called the grass tree because of the massed effect of its narrow leaflets. Yellow pea flowers in early summer. 3 × 2.4m/10 × 8ft

Deutzia × *elegantissima* **'Rosealind'**
One of the prettiest shrubs with clusters of
soft rose-pink flowers in early summer.
1 × 1.5m/3 × 5ft

Erysimum **'Bowles' Mauve'**
E: ○
Wonderful although short-
lived sub-shrubby
wallflower with blue-grey
foliage and mauve flowers
recurrently from spring to
autumn. 60 × 75cm/
2 × 2½ft

Cercis siliquastrum **(Judas tree)** ○
A very beautiful tree with heart-shaped blue-green
leaves and lilac-pink pea flowers in late spring/early
summer. Long, green-purple fruits follow on later in the
year. 10m/30ft H and W

× *Halimiocistus
wintonensis* **'Merrist Wood
Cream'** E: ○
A lovely shrub for a
prominent position, which
flowers profusely in late
spring or early summer.
Not always fully hardy.
60cm × 1.2m/2 × 4ft

Indigofera heterantha ○
An arching shrub with fern-like foliage and rich pink pea-flowers for a long period from summer to autumn. May be cut down in hard winters. 1.5m/5ft H and W

***Hibiscus syriacus* 'Blue Bird'** ○
A shrub that is late into leaf but spectacular in flower from late summer to mid autumn. Humus should be added to the soil. Given this, it will grow too in clay. 2.1m/7ft H and W

***Kolkwitzia amabilis* 'Pink Cloud'** ○
The beauty bush forms a large arching shrub massed with pink flowers like foxgloves in early summer. It has a peeling bark and leaves that turn reddish in autumn. 3m/10ft H and W

***Morus nigra* (Black mulberry)** ○
Picturesque in maturity, this spreading round-headed tree has heart-shaped leaves. The edible burgundy-red fruits are borne in late summer. Better placed on a lawn than paving, as they can make a mess when they fall. 12 × 15m/39 × 49ft

Paeonia delavayi ○
A shrub that has most beautiful grey-green foliage and gold-bossed maroon flowers for a short period in early summer. 1.8m/6ft H and W

Prunus tenella 'Firehill' ○
Showy flowers cluster along the stems of this small shrub in spring. This dwarf Russian almond is invaluable for its warm, bright colour early in the year. 1 × 1.2m/3 × 4ft

A SELECTION OF OTHER SHRUBS AND TREES FOR ALKALINE SOIL

Acer platanoides forms	*Liriodendron*
Acer pseudoplatanus forms	*Malus* (Crab) p.238
Amelanchier p.236	*Osmanthus*
Berberis p.90	*Paulownia*
Catalpa p.67	*Philadelphus* p.181
Ceanothus p.50	*Populus* (Poplar)
Cistus p.51	*Prunus* (Cherry)
Cornus p.64	*Pyrus* (Pear)
Cotoneaster p.126	*Quercus cerris*
Daphne p.75	*Romneya* p.147
Fagus (Beech) p.200	*Rosmarinus* p.115
Fraxinus excelsior (Ash)	*Taxus* (Yew) p.199
Gleditsia p.67	*Teucrium*
Hydrangea villosa p.124	*Viburnum* p.77
Koelreuteria paniculata p.241	*Weigela* p.93
	Yucca p.57
Laburnum p.209	

Santolina pinnata ssp. **neapolitana** E: ○
This cotton lavender makes a rounded shrub with aromatic grey-green foliage and yellow button flowers in summer. 75cm × 1m/2½ × 3ft

Xanthoceras sorbifolium ○
An elegant, unusual shrub with pinnate leaves and white, red-eyed flowers on spikes in late spring. 3 × 2.1m/10 × 7ft

Achillea filipendulina **'Gold Plate' (Yarrow)** ○
Dramatic flat heads of flowers in summer which are excellent for drying and will retain their colour well. 1.2m × 60cm/4 × 2ft

Achillea 'The Beacon' (syn. 'Fanal') ○
This form of yarrow is a useful coral-coloured alternative to the yellow cultivars. Summer-flowering. 75cm/2½ft H and W

Alyssum saxatile ○
A vigorous trailing perennial for a wall or rock garden. There is a pale lemon-yellow form called *A.s.* 'Citrinum'. 5 × 45cm/2in × 1½ft

Anthericum liliago **(St Bernard's lily)** ○
Delicate white stars rise on thin stems in early summer over clumps of glaucous, rushy leaves. The flowers are quite short-lived but they make a charming impact against a dark background. 60 × 45cm/2 × 1½ft

Asphodeline lutea (Yellow asphodel)
A rush-leafed perennial with spikes of starry flowers for
a long period in late spring to midsummer. Its glaucous
leaves and seed-heads make it decorative even after
flowering. 1m × 60cm/3 × 2ft

**Asplenium trichomanes
(Maidenhair spleenwort)**
A dwarf black-stemmed
fern that is often to be
found growing in the
crevices of stone steps.
10cm/4in H and W

Campanula garganica
A dwarf perennial with
starry flowers
successionally from
summer to autumn. Ideal
for walls or paving.
15 × 45cm/6in × 1½ft

Aubrieta deltoidea E: ○
A trailing carpeting perennial that will spill colour for a
long period in spring over walls or paving. Keep it
compact by cutting back hard after flowering.
5 × 45cm/2in × 1½ft

***Campanula glomerata
'Superba'*** ○
An easy vigorous perennial
bellflower that will gently
self-seed. Clusters of rich
blue flowers in summer
over soft green leaves.
60cm/2ft H and W

Centaurea cyanus **(Annual cornflower)** ○
Wonderful hardy annual which grows easily in any type
of soil. Blue, maroon or pink flowers on 45 × 30cm/
1½ × 1ft branching stems.

***Dianthus* 'Pike's Pink'** E:
○
One of the many scented
pinks which make cushions
for a rock garden or at the
front of a bed. 15cm/6in
H and W

Dictamnus albus purpureus (Burning bush)
A clump-forming perennial with spikes of pink or white flowers in summer. (The oils in the aromatic leaves can be set alight on hot days.) 75cm/2½ft H and W

Dracunculus vulgaris (Dragon arum) ○
A spreading tuberous perennial with dramatic spathes around a dark spadix in summer. They emit a foul smell after opening which fades after a couple of days. Not fully hardy. 1m × 45cm/3 × 1½ft

Euphorbia myrsinites ○
Trailing stems bear lime-yellow spring flowers. The fleshy blue-grey leaves make a decorative perennial at all times. Not fully hardy. 7.5 × 30cm/ 3in × 1ft

Echinops ritro ○
A stately perennial with globes of steel-blue heads in summer. 1.2m × 60cm/ 4 × 2ft

Galega orientalis ○
A bushy perennial which withstands hot dry conditions. It has spikes of pea flowers in early summer. 1.2m × 75cm/ 4 × 2½ft

Gypsophila 'Rosy Veil' ○
Tiny pink flowers in summer on wiry stems give a gauzy effect to this low-growing glaucous-leaved gypsophila. 45cm/ 1½ft H and W

Iberis (Candytuft) ○
A free-flowering dwarf hardy annual which is easy from seed, tolerates poor soil and will be a pretty gap-filler. 15cm/6in H and W

Linaria maroccana 'Fairy Bouquet' ○
A diminutive hardy annual which makes a charming summer filler in paving gaps. This dwarf toadflax is very easy from seed and gives a dainty effect. Its colour ranges from blue and violet to pink, red and yellow. 15cm/6in H and W

Linaria purpurea 'Canon Went' ○
The pink form of the usual purple type sending up thin spikes of tiny flowers in summer. It self-seeds gently. 60 × 30cm/2 × 1ft

***Lychnis coronaria* alba** ○
A short-lived silver-leafed perennial that self-seeds. This white form is less usual than the magenta *L. c. atrosanguinea.* 60 × 45cm/2 × 1½ft

A SELECTION OF OTHER PERENNIALS (INCLUDING BULBS) FOR ALKALINE SOIL

Acaena p.98
Acanthus spinosus p.54
Allium in variety
Anemone blanda p.128
Arabis
Campanula (most rock garden varieties) p.140
Campanula persicifolia
Coreopsis p.144
Crocus in variety p.135
Eryngium (some) p.54
Euphorbia polychroma p.60
Geranium p.102
Helenium p.168
Irises (most)
Linum narbonense p.145
Meconopsis cambrica p.217
Muscari
Pennisetum villosum
Pulsatilla vulgaris
Salvia nemorosa
Sidalcea p.165
Veronica rupestris
Viola labradorica p.91

***Origanum laevigatum* 'Hopley's Variety'** ○
A decorative marjoram with purple-pink bracts around tiny flowers that last for a long period in late summer. 30 × 45cm/ 1 × 1½ft

Scabiosa caucasica ○
The old-fashioned scabious produces its long thin stems of lovely large flowers in summer. 60cm/2ft H and W

Verbena bonariensis ○
An open, tall, branching perennial that gives an airy effect. It has clusters of mauve flowers in late summer. Self-seeding. 1.5m × 45cm/5 × 1½ft

Plants for Lime-free or Acid Soils

Some plants cannot thrive in alkaline soil, which is high in calcium. These calcifuges, which are often called lime-haters, become sickly unless they are planted in acid soil. Most ericaceous plants belong to this category and also some other examples which are slightly less lime-intolerant but still need neutral to acid soil. You can assess the kind of soil you have with a testing-kit that reveals whether it is alkaline, neutral or acid. If you have alkaline soil but want to grow a plant that needs acid or neutral soil, a possible solution is to grow it in a container.

Andromeda polifolia compacta E
The bog rosemary is a lovely small shrub with narrow glaucous leaves and pink flowers in late spring or early summer. For peaty soil. 30cm/1ft H and W

Calluna vulgaris 'Silver Knight' E: ○
Excellent ground cover in full sun. Lings flower midsummer to early autumn. 40cm × 1m/ 1ft 4in × 3ft

Cassiope 'Muirhead' E: ◑
Dwarf heath-like shrub with almost stemless bell flowers in spring on upright stems. 20cm/ 8in H and W

Embothrium coccineum (Chilean firebush) E or semi-E: ◑
Brilliant flowers in late spring, early summer on an erect shrub or small tree. Needs shelter as not fully hardy, though the cultivar called 'Norquinco' is somewhat hardier. All need rich, moist soil. 6 × 3m/20 × 10ft

Erica vagans 'Lyonesse' E: ○
This heather flowers in midsummer/autumn. It is very intolerant of drought. 75cm/2½ft H and W

Hamamelis × intermedia 'Jelena'
All witch hazels need lime-free soil. This is a distinctive form with clusters of coppery-red flowers. Good autumn leaf colour. 2.2 × 1.8m/7 × 6ft

Kalmia angustifolia rubra (Sheep laurel) E: ○
Deep rose flowers over a long period in summer on a slowly spreading bush. 75cm × 1m/2½ × 3ft

Kalmia latifolia 'Nimuck Red Bud' E
The calico bush, or mountain laurel, produces beautiful spring flowers a few years after planting. Full sun for maximum flowering (although it will grow well in part shade), moist rich soil. 3m/10ft H and W

Nyssa sylvatica (Tupelo) ○
Attractive slow-growing tree of pyramid form with
spectacular red and yellow autumn foliage. For sun
and moist soil. Resents disturbance, so plant the tree
when it is young. 16 × 12m/52 × 39ft

Pieris floribunda **'Forest
Flame'** E: ◑ ●
The red new foliage in
spring (later turning pink,
cream, finally green) needs
protection from late frosts.
4 × 1.8m/13 × 6ft

Sciadopitys verticillata
(Umbrella pine) E: ○
Distinctive slow-growing
conifer, conical in form,
with whorls of leaves like
umbrella spokes. For soil
which does not dry out.
12 × 4.5m/39 × 15ft

***Pieris japonica* 'Mountain Fire'** E:◑ ●
A neat compact form of this shrub with sprays of creamy bell flowers and stunning red shoots which hold their colour well. 1.5m/5ft H and W

***Rhododendron* 'Lem's Cameo'** E:◑
The flowers, pink in bud, appear mid-spring. Needs extra care and shelter lest the flowers are frosted. 1.8m/6ft H and W

OTHER SHRUBS AND TREES WHICH REQUIRE LIME-FREE SOIL

Callistemon citrinus 'Splendens'
Camellia p.50
Cornus canadensis p.104
Corylopsis pauciflora p.138
Enkianthus campanulatus p.125
Pernettya (Gaultheria) mucronata p.109
Fothergilla major p.125
Halesia carolina
H. monticola p.241
Hamamelis × intermedia 'Pallida' p.139
H. mollis
Leucothoe fontanesiana p.93
Lithodora diffusa p.109
Magnolia salicifolia p.237
M. × soulangeana p.237
Pinus radiata p.247
Rhododendron luteum p.77
Rhododendron (including azaleas) p.51

Tropaeolum speciosum ◑
A herbaceous twining climber with dazzling flowers in summer to autumn followed by bright blue fruits. Often grown over a dark-leafed host like yew. The roots must be shaded. 3m/10ft

SHRUBS AND TREES FOR LIME-FREE SOILS

39

Adiantum pedatum (Northern maidenhair fern) Semi E: ◗
Delicate fronds spray out on blackish stems. Slowly spreading rootstock. For moist soil and shelter as not fully hardy. 45cm/18in H and W

Adiantum venustum ◗
This exquisite maidenhair fern has pale green fronds. Not fully hardy so give it a sheltered position. For moist soil. 23 × 30cm/9 × 12in

Iris innominata E or semi-E
This beautiful beardless Pacific Coast iris produces its flowers in late spring to early summer. These come in a large variety of subtle colours: pink, blue, purple, cream, yellow, gold. 25cm/10in × indefinite spread

Gentiana sino-ornata E: ○
Rich blue trumpet flowers on a prostrate autumn-flowering gentian that thrives in moist soil. 5 × 30cm/2 × 12in

Lewisia cotyledon hybrid E: ○ ◑
Pink or purple flowers in early summer over rosettes of
leaves. Winter wet can rot the crown. Protect or plant
vertically in a rock crevice to prevent rain collecting in
the centre. 30 × 15cm/1ft × 6in

***Phlox adsurgens* 'Wagon
Wheel'** E: ◑
Showy wheel-like flowers
in summer on a mat-
forming plant that likes
peaty, gritty soil.
8 × 30cm/4 × 12in

Lilium pardalinum
The leopard lily flowers in summer with nodding
turkscap blooms. A vigorous bulb for moist soil which
may grow up to 2.1m/7ft.

***Phlox stolonifera* 'Ariane'**
E: ◐
Creeping perennial with milk white flowers in early summer over pale green leaves. Cut back after flowering. 30cm/1ft
H and W

Pleione formosana ◐
Tender bulb but in mild regions can be grown if protected in a very sheltered spot. Flowers on short stems just before the leaves grow in spring. 10cm/4in

Rhodohypoxis baurii ❍
Tubers producing pink, red or white flowers in summer. Only frost hardy if kept dry during its winter dormancy but enjoys moisture during its period of growth. 10 × 5cm/4 × 2in

Tricyrtis formosana
An autumn-flowering perennial with spreading rhizomes. Best in humus-rich soil that does not dry out. 60 × 45cm/2 × 1½ft

Trillium grandiflorum ●
The wake-robin forms a
clump and flowers in
spring. 40 × 30cm/
1ft 4in × 1ft

Trillium grandiflorum roseum ●
The ravishing pink form of the wake-robin also needs
moist but well-drained soil. Trilliums are also
sometimes called the trinity flower. 40 × 30cm/
1ft 4in × 1ft

Trillium sessile rubrum ●
Mahogany-red flowers in spring above mottled bronze-
green foliage. Give this lovely variety the same growing
conditions as the other wake-robins. 40 × 30cm/1ft 4in ×
1ft

OTHER PERENNIALS FOR
LIME-FREE SOIL

Blechnum tabulare p.88
Erythronium p.129
Kirengeshoma palmata
 p.169
Lilium speciosum rubrum
Meconopsis betonicifolia
 p.169
Meconopsis × *sheldonii*
Smilacina racemosa
 p.111

Designing with Plants

When you design a garden, it is your choice of plants that will help give it form, colour, scent and ease of maintenance. For example, beautiful foliage plants will provide interest when the flowers die away and evergreens will give it a winter structure. Scented plants will entice you into the garden and groundcover subjects will reduce your weeding.

Evergreens

It is a cardinal rule that evergreens should form the backbone of a garden, and this is especially true in the area near the house. These are the plants that will keep the garden looking clothed in winter in a northern climate and if they are neglected here, particularly, you will be looking out at a bare area of masonry for half the year.

The best possible use of evergreens is to place them with a view to their collective appearance when all else has withered around them in winter. Don't bunch them all together but space them out around the boundaries, in the corners, near the house and at the furthest point from the house. In this way, you can ensure that the garden looks dressed even in the bleakest months. Vary the type of evergreens, too; choose small as well as tall subjects, conifers but also broad-leafed shrubs, and both delicate and bold-foliaged plants. Supplement the list with evergreen climbers (pages 220–229), with evergreens from gold and bright green plants (pages 60–67) and those plants which have been marked with an E throughout the book.

Dryas octopetala
(**Mountain avens**) E: ○
Mat-forming shrub with oak-like leaves, shining green above, and white, yellow-centred flowers in early summer. 10 × 37cm/ 4in × 1ft 3in

× *Fatshedera lizei* E
Shade-tolerant, glossy-leaved plant which is a cross between *Fatsia japonica* and ivy. Lax-growing stems make spreading, prostrate ground-cover or they can be tied to supports to form a shrub up to 2.1m/7ft.

Lonicera pileata E: ◑ ●
A small ground-cover
shrub with glossy box-like
leaves and small creamy
flowers in late spring,
followed by purple berries.
60cm × 1.8m/2 × 6ft

Iberis sempervirens E: ○
Vigorous, spreading dark green mats covered with milk-
white flowers in spring. 'Snowflake' is a good form of
this popular sub-shrub. 15 × 60cm/6in × 2ft

Mossy saxifrage E: ◑
Pretty, accommodating, enthusiastic carpeters for semi-
shade where they will prefer moist soil but endure dry;
'Triumph' has blood-red flowers in late spring. 'Gaiety'
is rose pink; 'Pearly King' is white.
15 × 45cm+/6 in × 1½ft+

Azara lanceolata E
A wall shrub or small tree with fanning branches of minute dark green leaves. It bears small, yellow, scented flowers in late spring. It is not fully hardy. 5m/16ft H and W

Choisya ternata E
A shrub with shining, dark green leaves and fragrant, small white flowers in clusters in late spring and sometimes autumn too. Sun or shade. Give wall shelter in very cold or draughty areas. Spreading growth. 2.1 × 3m/7 × 10ft

Prunus laurocerasus (**Laurel**) E
Shade-tolerant shrub with white flowers in spring and glossy green leaves. Will reach 6m/20ft if free-growing but can be clipped hard to form a screen. Its most distinctive form is 'Otto Luyken', which has a low domed habit and narrow leaves.

Lonicera nitida E
Tiny darkest green leaves on a shrub much used for hedging, though it needs cutting up to four times a year as a hedge. Grow at 30cm/1ft intervals to form a barrier. The yellow-leafed cultivar 'Baggesen's Gold' makes an excellent specimen in part-shade. 4m/13ft H and W

Juniperus **'Pfitzeriana Aurea'** E
Wide-spreading shrub with strong, ascending branches and gold-green foliage. Very popular and much used to give pronounced, horizontal effects to a design; also useful for its ground-covering, weed-smothering capacity. There is a grey-green form ('Pftizeriana Glauca'), and a smaller form ('Compacta') for those who do not have room for the type plant. 1.8 × 4m/6 × 13ft

Abies koreana E
Compact fir with leaves which are dark green above and white beneath. 6cm/2½in violet-deep blue cones are freely produced even on young trees. 9 × 4.5m/30 × 15ft

Pinus mugo **(Mountain Pine)** E: ○
Stiff, deep green needles and very small cones on a dense, bushy shrub with spreading habit. Good on poor, limy soils. Slow-growing to 3 × 5m/ 10 × 16ft.

CONSIDER ALSO: conifers on pages 240–1.

Taxus baccata E
The yew is an immensely adaptable tree, used greatly for hedges, for topiary or as a specimen. A free-growing yew would be too large and funereal for a garden, but in a formal setting, several clipped into a neat shape could be suitable. Sun or shade. Size according to pruning.

Tsuga canadensis **'Pendula'** E: ◑ ●
Bizarre in growth, this is the low, mounded, weeping form of the eastern hemlock. It tolerates alkaline soil, but prefers moist but well-drained neutral to acid soil. Very slow to 1.8–2.4m/6–8ft or more.

Camellia E: LH: ◗
These are a first choice for soil which is neutral to acid. There are two main hardy varieties, *C. japonica* and *C. × williamsii*; the former retains dead flowers, the latter drops them. 'Leonard Messel' (above) is a beautiful hybrid of the *C. × williamsii* group, a vigorous, erectly-branched bush, with the glossy leaves common to all camellias. Its flowers are pink with deeper veins, produced in spring. 4 × 3m/13 × 10ft

Carpenteria californica E: ○
Dazzling display of white fragrant flowers in midsummer on a rounded shrub with rich glossy foliage. Needs a sheltered position and rich, moist though well-drained soil. 1.5m/5ft H and W

Ceanothus E: ○ in variety.
An invaluable (mainly evergreen) group. 'Delight' has rich blue, scented panicles of flowers in late spring, on an erect, fairly hardy bush. 'Cascade' (shown above) is a more tender cultivar with arching growth. *C. impressus* 'Puget Blue' is amongst the best for warmer areas. Autumn-flowering varieties include the tender 'Burkwoodii' and 'Autumnal Blue', which is one of the hardiest. Full sun and good drainage essential. Wall shelter is important, except in warm areas. 2.5m/8ft H and W

Cistus 'Peggy Sammons'
E: ○
A floriferous summer-flowering shrub for light dry soil and full sun. It has grey-green soft foliage and charming pink flowers. It is not fully hardy. 1m/3ft H and W.

Consider also *Cistus × cyprius*, *C. × pulverulentus* and *C. × purpureus*.

Hebe E
A group of New Zealand shrubs the finest of which are unfortunately rather tender. The photograph shows *Hebe* 'Simon Delaux' with dark, glossy leaves and purplish-red flower spikes from late summer to autumn; 1.5 × 1m/5 × 3ft. It is a hybrid of *H. speciosa*, like the following fine cultivars; 'Alicia Amherst' (purple-blue), 'Purple Queen' and the magenta-purple 'La Séduisante'. *H. hulkeana* has very long mauve-blue flower panicles in early summer. Hardier varieties include the bronze-leafed, violet-flowered 'Mrs. Winder', and the bright pink 'Great Orme'. 1–1.5m/3–5ft

Ozothamnus ledifolius E: ○
A bushy aromatic and stiff-leafed shrub with small white honey-scented flowers, orange in bud, in early summer. Not fully hardy. 1m/3ft H and W

Rhododendrons and azaleas E: LH: ◗
These provide a vast and magnificent variety of flowering evergreens, though only for acid soil. The small cultivars are of most general use but nearly all demand part shade. *R.* 'Elizabeth' with rich red trumpet flowers in spring is shown here; 1 × 1.5m/3 × 5ft.

Architectural Plants

Bold-leafed plants are of great architectural value and provide points of reference in an otherwise fussy background. They have the advantage of standing out against stones underfoot, looming walls and perhaps the back of a house too, against an environment which would dominate nearly all other kinds of plants. For these reasons, it is a good idea to include in a garden those flowers and shrubs which are striking in leaf or habit for a good proportion of the year. Evergreens are the most useful of these, for they have a continuous part to play; but herbaceous plants with a definite outline to their foliage are equally valuable, partly because their presence (and absence) in different seasons changes the appearance of the scene. A garden which contains a high proportion of such plants will look shapely, and not simply a collection of oddments.

Alchemilla mollis
Lime-yellow flower-sprays in summer over a mound of leaves. It is a prodigious seeder so remove the flowering stems before seeds ripen. 45cm/1½ft H and W

Bergenia cordifolia E
Glossy, evergreen leaves and magenta flowers in spring. *B.c.* 'Purpurea' has leaves which turn purple-red in winter. Hybrids include 'Ballawley' (shown here) with rosy-red flowers; and 'Silberlicht' with white flowers. 45cm/1½ft H and W

Ferns ◑
Athyrium filix-femina is a deciduous, light green native fern. *A.f.f. plumosum* is a more feathery cultivar and *A.f.f.* 'Victoriae' has crested ends. 75×45cm/ $2^1/_2 \times 1^1/_2$ft *Dryopteris borreri cristata* is a graceful, evergreen fern with crests and a stiff, imposing habit.

Helleborus argutifolius
(syn. *corsicus*) E
Deeply-cut dark, evergreen leaves with icy green flowers in spring. Vigorous and tolerant of even dry shade. 60cm/2ft H and W

Hosta sieboldiana ◑
Large, blue-grey leaves and lilac flower spikes in summer on one of the most magnificent perennials, making a stately mound. *H.s.* 'Elegans' has bluer leaves. 90×45cm/$3 \times 1^1/_2$ft

***Acanthus spinosus* (Bear's breeches)**
Mauve and white hooded flowers in later summer rise above glossy leaves.
120 × 60cm/4 × 2ft

***Crocosmia* 'Lucifer'** ○
A bulb with arching, red crests in summer above sword-like leaves. 'Citronella' is soft yellow. Soil must not dry out. 60 × 15cm/2ft × 6in

***Eryngium giganteum* (Sea holly)** ○
Self-sowing biennial with silver-blue thistles, silver bracts and spiny leaves. It makes a good subject for cutting and drying. It is tolerant of dry soil.
1m × 30cm/3 × 1ft

Eryngium agavifolium E
This perennial sea holly has narrow spiny leaves and green flower heads.
1.2m × 45cm/4 × 1½ft

Euphorbia characias ssp. ***wulfenii* (Spurge)** E
A bold, shrubby euphorbia which needs a position
sheltered from buffeting winds. Dark, bluish-green
leaves and lime-yellow bottle-brush heads all spring.
90cm × 1.2m/3 × 4ft

***Kniphofia* (Red-hot poker)** hybrids ○
Most have grassy foliage and the best include 'Little
Maid' (shown above) with creamy poker heads late
summer to autumn. 60 × 45cm/2 × 1¹/₂ft

Kniphofia northiae E
This poker has exotic, glaucous, broad leaves in
rosettes and cream and red flower spikes in summer.
1m/3ft H and W

***Cynara cardunculus* (Cardoon)** ○
A stately silver candelabra whose giant purple thistle-heads in summer can be eaten in soups, its stalks blanched and cooked. 2.1 × 1m/7 × 3ft

***Cynara scolymus* (Globe artichoke)** ○
A shorter version of the cardoon, whose violet thistle-heads can be eaten before flowering in summer. 1.8m × 75cm/ 6 × 2½ft

***Cordyline australis* (New Zealand cabbage palm)** E
In mild areas, this will develop into a small tree with a bunch of green sword-like leaves crowning each branch and creamy flower panicles in early summer. When juvenile, forms a grassy fountain from a central stem. Tender and it will require protection in winter. Ultimately 8m/26ft where it thrives, otherwise 1.5m/5ft.

Trachycarpus fortunei E
Slow-growing but hardy
Chusan palm with fan-
shaped leaves. Will give a
sub-tropical appearance to
its surroundings.
Ultimately 11 × 5m/
36 × 16ft.

Yucca gloriosa E: ○
Thick, grey, spiky and
spine-tipped leaf-mounds
topped in hot summer by
a 2m/6¹/₂ft spire of cream
bell-flowers. *Y. recurvifolia*
is equally tall, but *Y.
filamentosa* with hair-like
threads on its leaves and
the similar but limp-leafed
Y. flaccida are smaller.

Onopordum arabicum ○
Magnificent silver biennial flowering in summer when
it reaches to 1.8m/6ft. *O. acanthium* is taller at
2.5–3m × 60cm/8–10 × 2ft. Both self-sow invasively and
have sharp spines on their leaves, so may not be suitable
in a garden with children.

Fatsia japonica E: ◑
Handsome, glossy dark evergreen leaves on a spreading
bush which bears creamy flower-heads in late autumn
followed by small black fruits. 2.1 × 2.4m/7 × 8ft

Mahonia japonica E: ◑
Shade-bearing evergreen with spiky, dark leaves and
lily-of-the-valley-scented, lemon-yellow flowers which
appear in early spring. Best in moist soil. 1.8m × 3m/
6 × 10ft

Mahonia lomariifolia E
Rather more tender than its relative and therefore
better placed in a nook between sunny walls in cold
areas. Leggy habit, each stem crowned with dark
evergreen leaves and crests of yellow flowers in late
autumn or winter. 3m × 1.8m/10 × 6ft

Viburnum rhytidophyllum E
Vigorous evergreen shrub with wrinkled leaves, dark green on top and grey beneath; cream flowers in late spring followed by red berries which turn black. Only for very large areas, as shrubs of both sexes must be grouped to ensure fruit. 3 × 3.5m/10 × 12ft

Phormium tenax (**New Zealand flax**) E: ○
Clump-forming, sword-leafed evergreen perennial forming a dramatic feature. The type has greyish-green leaves topped by a 3.5m/12ft dark red flower spike in summer. Cultivars with purple leaves, or with variegated leaves ranging from cream to dark bronze are available. Not fully hardy. 1.8 × 1m/6 × 3ft

Viburnum plicatum '**Mariesii**'
Tiers of horizontal branches covered in white lace-cap flowers during early summer. Deciduous though the layers of bare branches are distinctive even in winter. 1.8 × 2.1m/6 × 7ft

Gold and Bright Green Plants

It is in the dark and gloomy garden that a mixture of gold and light, bright green leaves comes into its own: golden evergreens and yellow-flowered or -fruited plants are an invaluable way of adding brightness to a dreary winter scene, and gold and green additions will give the impression of soft sunshine on a dull day at any time of the year.

Take care about the kind of flowers you introduce in this setting. Orange and yellow flowers will reinforce the illumination brilliantly. White blossom will cool the brightness. Blue flowers will always seem fresh against golden foliage; this combination is contrasting yet harmonious in a green setting, for green is a secondary colour formed by these two primaries. But never introduce flowers of mixed strong colours in a golden setting for they will simply make it garish.

**Carex elata 'Aurea'
(Bowles' golden sedge)** E:
○
The leaves of this showy sedge will be brighter in some sun. It requires moist soil. 60cm/2ft H and W

Euphorbia polychroma
Lime-yellow flower heads all spring over bright green leaves which turn pinker in autumn. This attractive spurge is shown here amongst forget-me-nots. 45cm/1½ft H and W

Hosta 'Gold Standard' ◐
A first class vigorous hosta with gold leaves edged finely
with dark green. Forms a good clump and retains its
colour well. Lavender flowers in summer. 60cm/2ft
H and W

Milium effusum **'Aureum'**
◐
Bowles' golden grass has
gold leaves, stems and
flowers. Pretty with spring
flowers. Self-sowing.
45×30cm/$1\frac{1}{2} \times 1$ft

CONSIDER ALSO:

Hakonechloa macra
  'Alba-aurea' p.173
Origanum vulgare
  'Aureum'
Thymus 'Doone Valley'

Melissa officinalis **'Aurea'** ◐
A lemon balm with gold-variegated, aromatic leaves.
Keep clipping to promote new yellow leaves. Useful
herb, best in semi-shade. 60×45cm/$2 \times 1\frac{1}{2}$ft

Valeriana phu **'Aurea'** ○
A perennial with brilliant golden foliage in early
spring which turns to green in summer. Its white
flowers which are insignificant appear at the same
time. 20×30cm/8in $\times$ 1ft

***Hedera helix* 'Buttercup' (Ivy)** E: ◖
A beautiful form with soft yellow leaves that need at least part-sun to retain their colour. They will green in full shade. 2.7m/9ft

Other golden or gold and green ivies include *Hedera helix* 'Goldheart' (above), *H.h.* 'Angularis Aurea' and *H. colchica* 'Sulphur Heart'.

***Humulus lupulus* 'Aureus'** ○
A vigorous, golden-leafed hop which grows and colours best in full sun but needs a moist though well-drained position. It is a herbaceous twiner with yellow-green flower bracts. 4m/13ft

***Lonicera japonica* 'Aureo-reticulata'** Semi-E
Fairly vigorous, semi-evergreen honeysuckle with a network of golden veins on its green leaves. Flowers sparsely midsummer onwards, its blooms varying from white through yellow with a purple stain. 5m/16ft

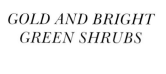

Acer shirasawanum f. ***aureum*** **(Golden leafed Japanese maple)**
A beautiful shrub which requires some shelter. In hot dry situations its rounded, pale yellow leaves are liable to suffer sun-scorch. 3 × 2.4m/10 × 8ft

Berberis thunbergii **'Aurea'** ◑
Dazzling yellow in new growth, this neat shrub fades to yellow-green later. It may scorch in full sun. 75cm/2½ft H and W

Aucuba japonica **'Gold Dust'** E
A valuable statuesque plant, dense and bushy, with red berries that are held on the shrub from autumn until spring. 2.4m/8ft H and W

63

Cornus alba 'Aurea'
A handsome dogwood with maroon stems and
golden-green leaves. Insignificant white flowers in
summer. 3m/10ft H and W

Choisya ternata 'Sundance' E
A brilliant yellow form of the Mexican orange-blossom
with scented white flowers in late spring. Not fully hardy
and needs a sheltered position. 1.5 × 1.8m/5 × 6ft

Elaeagnus pungens 'Dicksonii' E: ○
A bushy vigorous shrub with glossy leaves that have
large central splashes of gold. 2.4 × 3m/8 × 10ft.
E. × ebbingei 'Gilt Edge' has foliage with a golden
margin. Both shrubs have small fragrant flowers in
autumn.

***Euonymus fortunei* 'Emerald 'n Gold'** E
Brilliant low and spreading bush, staining pink in
winter; valuable ground-cover for sun or shade. Climbs
if supported. 60cm × 1m/2 × 3ft

***Ilex aquifolium* E**
There are many gold variegated forms including
'Golden Queen' which has bright golden yellow margins
to its spiny leaves. It is male, despite its name, so does
not produce fruit. 3m/10ft H and W

***Ligustrum ovalifolium* 'Aureum'** E: ○
The bright golden privet which is at its best when
hard-clipped into a compact shape to prevent
gappiness at the base. 1.5m+/5ft+ H and W

Taxus baccata 'Aurea' E
A yew of soft gold which
will revert to greener tones
if grown in heavy shade.
6 × 5m/20 × 16ft. Other
yellow yews include the
shorter, spreading
'Semperaurea' and a slow-
growing Irish yew,
'Standishii', forming a slim
column to about 1.2m/4ft.

CONSIDER ALSO:

Juniperus chinensis
  'Aurea' p.246
Juniperus 'Pfitzeriana
  Aurea' p.49
Lonicera nitida
  'Baggesen's Gold'
  p.48

Sambucus racemosa 'Plumosa Aurea'
This shrub has beautiful foliage with scarlet berries in
summer after yellow flower-heads. It grows best in part-
shade to avoid scorching. Moist soil is necessary. 3m/10ft
H and W

Catalpa bignonioides 'Aurea'
Bright copper leaves when new, turning yellow as they age and then greener later in the season. Not for exposed places. Spreading habit. 8m/26ft H and W

Gleditsia triacanthos 'Sunburst' ○
Bright yellow ferny leaves, greening later, on spreading branches. Fast-growing but best in sheltered positions. Can be pruned in spring to keep tree smaller and induce a burst of young foliage. 12m/40ft H and W

Robinia pseudoacacia 'Frisia'
Bright gold pinnate leaves all summer, but tinting a warmer apricot in autumn. Fast-growing and not for exposed positions. It is one of the most eye-catching of trees for the garden. 12 × 8m/40 × 26ft

Grey and Silver Plants

Leaves in these shades act as a foil to all other colours, whether rich or pastel, primary or secondary. But a silver area or border has in its own right a shimmering effect, seen at its most brilliant against a sombre background such as a deep green or purple-leafed hedge. Here, it will glow especially at dusk, a time of day when the deeper greens of the garden have melted into the darkness.

Not all silver plants are bone hardy (many have their origins in the Mediterranean region), but they do have a practical advantage. Hailing from these hot, dry parts, most are well adapted to drought, a great boon if watering the garden in summer proves difficult.

Grow most of the plants in sun, but the very few that will tolerate shade will make a dark corner gleam with light. The foliage of the plants shown below varies between white, silver, grey, grey-green and near blue. The texture of the leaves is also remarkable for its variety; some are lacy, others furry or felted.

***Artemisia absinthium*
'Lambrook Silver'** E: ○
Bush with delicate silver-blue leaves. Spikes of creamy flowers in summer; remove these to induce fresh foliage. 60 × 45cm/ 2 × 1½ft

***Dicentra* 'Langtrees'**
A robust spreading perennial with finely cut grey-green leaves and sprays of pearly flowers in late spring and early summer. 45cm/1½ft H and W

***Dicentra* 'Stuart Boothman'**
A lovely perennial with filigree steel blue foliage and sprays of pink pendant flowers in spring to early summer. 30 × 45cm/1 × 1½ft

***Artemisia ludoviciana*
(White sage)** ○
A clump-forming perennial with silver foliage which is at its most dazzling before the spikes of tiny pale flowers form in summer. 1.2m × 60cm/ 4 × 2ft

Festuca ovina E
Spreading hummocks of
blue-grey grass and sprays
of small fawn flowers in
early summer. May need
dividing every few years.
Planted closely it can be
clipped or mown like a
lawn. 25 × 22cm in
flower/10 × 9in

***Hosta* 'Halcyon'** ◑ ●
A compact plant with neat heart-shaped leaves of a
gunmetal blue. Lavender flowers are borne on stems in
summer. For moist soils. 45cm/1½ft H and W

Stachys byzantina (syn. *S.
olympica*) E: ○
Old cottage favourite with
very furry silvery leaves,
giving it the common
name of lamb's ears. Pink
flowers on spiky stems in
summer. Self-sowing.
45cm/1½ft in flower
(× 30cm/1ft). 'Silver
Carpet' is a non-flowering
cultivar.

Nepeta* × *faassenii ○
Catmint is an easy plant,
much used for ground-
cover and edging, with
greeny-grey leaves (often
eaten back to the quick by
cats) and mauve-blue
spikes all summer.
45cm/1½ft H and W

Paeonia mlokosewitschii
Mounds of soft grey-green leaves make this peony of
foliage value but, for a brief period in early summer, its
soft lemon single flowers with golden stamens give it
exceptional beauty. 60cm/2ft H and W

Convolvulus cneorum E: ○
A shrub with pale pink and white flowers in early
summer and brilliant silver lanceolate leaves. Not
reliably hardy and needs shelter. 60cm/2ft H and W

CONSIDER ALSO:

Acaena 'Blue Haze p.98
Antennaria dioica 'Rosea'
   p.98
Anthemis cupaniana
   p.214
Cardoon p.56
Cerastium tomentosum
   'Silver Carpet' p.98
Dianthus arenarius
D. gratianopolitanus
   p.116
Geranium ×
   riversleaianum 'Russell
   Prichard'
Globe artichoke p.56
Hebe albicans
H. pagei
*Helictotrichon
   sempervirens* p.86
Hosta sieboldiana p.53
Juniperus communis
   'Hibernica' p.246
J. virginiana 'Skyrocket'
   p.246
Lamium 'Beacon Silver'
Onopordum acanthium
O. arabicum p.57
Othonna cheirifolia p.99
Romneya coulteri p.147
Rosa glauca p.91
Tanacetum densum subsp.
   amani p.99
Thymus lanuginosus
Verbascum olympicum
Veronica incana
Yucca p.57

Helichrysum angustifolium (syn. *italicum*) E: ○
This aromatic shrub has narrow leaves and is spindly
but worth inclusion for its powerful scent of curry. Gold
flower clusters on white stems in summer. 60cm/2ft
H and W

***Lavandula angustifolia*
'Hidcote'** E: ○
A lavender that bears
flowers of an intense violet
45cm/1½ft H and W.
'Munstead' lavender has
mauve flowers, a compact
cultivar to 60cm/2ft. Dutch
lavender forms the biggest
bush to 1.2m/4ft. White
and pink-flowered
cultivars are sometimes
available. The form with
the whitest foliage is called
Lavandula lanata but good
drainage is essential.

***Ruta graveolens* 'Jackman's Blue'** E: ○
Opalescent blue-grey foliage which is beautiful and
filigree but may cause dermatitis in some gardeners,
Remove yellow flowers in summer in order to keep the
shrub compact. 60cm/2ft H and W

Santolina chamaecyparissus E: ○
The cotton lavender bears palest grey leaves on the
plant which should be kept shrubby and compact by
being hard-pruned in spring. Yellow button flowers in
summer. 60cm/2ft H and W

Salix helvetica
A small twiggy shrub for moist soil with glossy grey
leaves and grey then yellow upright catkins in spring.
60 × 45cm/2 × 1½ft

Brachyglottis (*syn. Senecio*)
'Sunshine' E: ○
Lax-growing and very
spreading shrub with
silver-grey-green leaves
and yellow daisy flowers in
summer. Good subject for
banks because of its
tumbling coverage.
1 × 1.2m/3 × 4ft

Buddleja davidii 'Nanho Blue' ○
Soft grey-green foliage and lavender spikes of flowers in
late summer on a shrub which is not quite as quick-
growing or large as other buddlejas. 1.8 × 2.1m/6 × 7ft.
B. 'Lochinch' has paler grey foliage and *B. crispa* has
woolly silvery leaves.

Cytisus battandieri ○
The immensely vigorous though not fully hardy
Moroccan broom with silky silvery trifoliate leaves and
large golden flower heads in summer, smelling like
ripe pineapples. 4 × 5m/13 × 16ft

Elaeagnus angustifolia (Oleaster) ○
Bushy shrub or small tree with penetratingly fragrant
tiny beige flowers in early summer followed by small
yellow fruits. 5 × 3.5m/16 × 12ft

Hippophae rhamnoides ○
Silver-grey linear leaves on
a large shrub which makes
one of the best supports
for clematis. The female
produces a mass of orange
berries if a male plant is
placed nearby. 5m/16ft
H and W

Perovskia atriplicifolia ○
A rather lax-growing shrub with finely cut grey leaves
and lavender blue flowers late in the summer. Prune in
spring. 1m/3ft H and W

Pyrus salicifolia 'Pendula'
Unique weeping pear tree
with narrow silver leaves
and small cream flowers in
spring. Grows vigorously
to form a mushroom-
shaped head. 8 × 6m/
26 × 20ft

Rosa × alba 'Celestial'
Vigorous and healthy
summer-blooming old rose
forming a tall shrub of
grey-green leaves.
Exquisite shell-pink roses
with the sweetest scent.
Will tolerate half shade.
1.8m/6ft H and W

Sorbus aria 'Lutescens'
A whitebeam making a handsome tree with silver leaves
in spring, turning grey-green in summer. Clusters of
white flowers in late spring to early summer are
followed by orange-red fruits in autumn. 10 × 8m/
33 × 26ft

Scented Plants

Fragrance is an unseen dimension to plants, invisible but nonetheless very potent. Some plants are imbued with it so that each part carries the scent, whereas in other plants only the flowers are perfumed. A number emit so pervasive a scent that it can be smelt twenty yards away whilst others release their volatile oils only when rubbed or brushed.
It will give you the greatest pleasure if you can grow a few of the sweeter scented plants near the house so that their fragrance becomes a constant companion. Alternatively an ideal way of growing these plants is to put them in an enclosure which will intensify their scent.

Buddleja globosa Semi-E: ○
Honey scented small orange globes are produced in late spring to early summer. 1.8 × 1.2m/ 6 × 4ft

Choisya 'Aztec Pearl' E: ○
A more compact pretty relative of the Mexican orange blossom (*C. ternata*) with finely cut leaves. Flowers profusely in late spring. 1.2 × 1m/4 × 3ft

Daphne × burkwoodii 'Somerset' Semi-E
All daphnes are heavily scented. This hybrid forms a dome and blooms in late spring. Further flowers are sometimes produced in the autumn. 75cm/2½ft H and W

Daphne cneorum 'Eximia' E: ○
Prostrate shrub massed with exquisitely scented starry flowers in late spring. 10 × 60cm/4in × 2ft

Magnolia grandiflora 'Exmouth' E: ○
Best grown against a wall in cold areas. The large waxy flowers, like waterlilies, open in late summer. Handsome leathery foliage. 4m/13ft + on a wall

Euphorbia mellifera E: ○
Honey scented inflorescence in early summer on a handsome foliage shrub. Not fully hardy and apt to be cut down in hard winters. 1.2 × 1m/4 × 3ft

Lonicera fragrantissima ○
Twiggy shrub with creamy waxy flowers in late winter to early spring, followed by red berries. 1.8m/6ft H and W

Magnolia wilsonii ◖
Beautiful fragrant but
fleeting saucer flowers in
late spring on a shrubby
tree. 4 × 2.4m/13 × 8ft

Matthiola fruticulosa alba ○
The perennial white stock has wonderfully scented
flowers in late spring and glistening grey leaves. Short-
lived but valuable. 60cm/2ft H and W

***Philadelphus* 'Sybille'** ○
One of the loveliest small
mock oranges. Flowering
in summer, it has a
spreading habit and
purple-flushed blossom.
1.2m/4ft H and W

Poncirus trifoliata ◖
The Japanese bitter orange has sparse sharply spined
twigs and sweetly scented flowers in late spring followed
by tangerine-like fruits. 1.8m/6ft H and W

Rhododendron luteum (*Azalea pontica*) LH
Rich golden flowers in late spring emit a penetrating
honey scent for a distance. Good autumn leaf colouring.
Like most rhododendrons it should be grown in acid or
lime-free soil. 2.4m/8ft H and W

**Viburnum × bodnantense
'Dawn'** ○
Deep rose pink buds open
into paler, scented flowers
from autumn to early
spring. A valuable plant
for the winter garden.
1.5 × 1.8m/5 × 6ft

Syringa meyeri 'Palibin' (*S. velutina* or *S. palibiana*) ○
Excellent twiggy lilac for the small garden flowering in
late spring. The fragrant flowers are borne in dense
panicles. 1.2 × 1m/4 × 3ft

***Rosa* 'Constance Spry'** ○
A modern rose which is
only once-flowering
though the display of
cabbage-rose blooms is
dazzling. Scented of
myrrh. May need support
and can be grown on a
wall. To 1.8m/6ft

***Rosa* 'Fragrant Cloud'** ○
Large heavily perfumed flowers are freely produced
on this vigorous hybrid tea rose. The habit of this
shrub is upright and it is well covered with mid-green
foliage. 1m/3ft H and W

All Gallica roses (old French roses) are perfumed. This is
'Charles de Mills', wine coloured and sumptuous. Its
formation is distinctive, as the bloom has a flat, sliced-off
appearance. Once flowering. Best in sun. 1.2m/4ft H
and W

Rosa **'Penelope'** ○
One of the best hybrid musk roses whose luscious
creamy pink flowers are produced over a very long
period. 1.5m/5ft H and W

Lonicera periclymenum **'Belgica'**
The scented 'Early Dutch Honeysuckle'
flowers in summer. The later form, *L.p.*
'Serotina', is equally fragrant, slightly
darker hued. Shade the roots. 5m/16ft

Wisteria sinensis **'Caroline'** ○
One of the best scented forms flowering
at an early stage of its life (in late spring)
and magnificently. 15m/48ft

OTHER SHRUBS AND
CLIMBERS WITH
FRAGRANT FLOWERS:

Azara lanceolata p.48
Brugmansia p.151
Buddleja davidii p.180
Carpenteria californica
    p.50
Ceanothus p.50
Chimonanthus fragrans
Clematis armandii p.222
C. balearica p.138
Cytisus battandieri p.72
Daphne odora
    'Aureomarginata'
    p.138
Elaeagnus angustifolia
    p.72
Jasminum officinale
    p.148
Magnolia salicifolia
    p.237
Mahonia japonica p.58
Osmanthus delavayi
Roses
Viburnum × juddii p.121

79

SCENTED ANNUALS,
BIENNIALS,
PERENNIALS AND
BULBS

Convallaria majalis ◑ ●
The lily of the valley, a
rhizomatous perennial not
always easy to establish but
spreading by runners
where happy. 8in/
20cm × indefinite

Cheiranthus cheiri (**Wallflower**) ○
Scented, spring-bedding biennial plants in flame,
primrose, brown, blood-red, pink, purple or ruby.
15–45 × 15–30cm/6in–1½ft × 6in–1ft

80

Cosmos atrosanguineus ❍
Velvet flowers from
summer to autumn with
chocolate scent on a
perennial that is not fully
hardy. 45cm/1¹/₂ft H and W

Dianthus barbatus (**Sweet William**) ❍
Scented flowers for summer of white, pink, scarlet or
crimson on this easy biennial. 45–60 × 30cm/
1¹/₂–2ft × 1ft. There is also a dwarf variety which can be
grown as an annual.

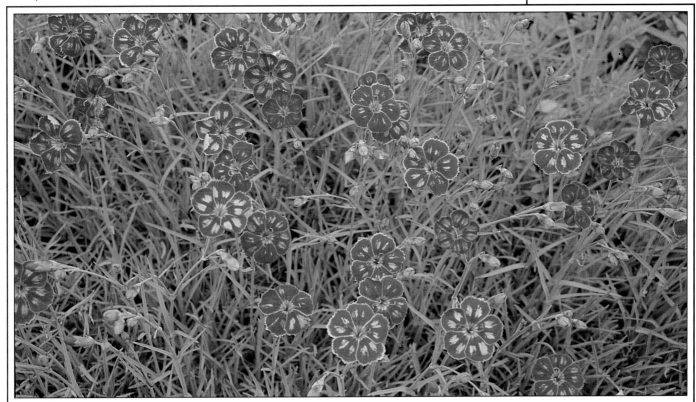

***Dianthus* 'Gravetye Gem'** E: ❍
Most pinks are scented. This one is clove-sweet and a
sound perennial, spreading slowly into a cushion of
densely packed blue-grey leaves. Summer-flowering. 15
× 30cm/6 × 12in

Hemerocallis lilio-asphodelus
Day lily flowering in late spring to early summer with sweet-scented trumpets and rushy leaves. 60cm/2ft H and W

Hesperis matronalis
The sweet rocket produces white or mauve heads of blossom in late spring. Self-sows gently. The double form is sought-after but trickier.
75 × 45cm/2¹/₂ × 1¹/₂ft

Hyacinthus orientalis **(Hyacinth)**
Stiff and formal bulb in habit but loved for its overpowering fragrance in spring. As shown here, it is a popular subject for formal spring bedding. 20cm/8in

Lilium **'Pink Perfection'**
Voluptuously scented trumpet flowers in summer on a
bulb that grows to 1.2m/4ft or more. Grow it in a pot so
that it can be placed in an appropriate position in the
garden. Here it is shown in front of white hydrangeas.

Matthiola **(Stock)** ○
There are annual stocks, but the biennial is the
Brompton stock, branching plants in shades of white,
pink, carmine, mauve or purple with a rich scent. The
flowering time is early summer. 45 × 37cm/1¹/₂ft × 1ft 3in

Narcissus tazetta ○
A variable species,
blooming from late autumn
to mid-spring. The well-
known tender 'Paper
White', with glistening
white very fragrant flowers
often forced for winter, is a
cultivar. Jonquils, another
group of narcissi, are also
very scented. Of the double
daffodils, 'Sir Winston
Churchill' (white with
orange florets) is fragrant
and a good garden plant.

Chamaemelum nobile ○
Chamomile, a ground cover plant, is sometimes
substituted for grass as a small lawn. The form
'Treneague' does not flower. Best in light soil. 15cm/6in
H and W

Mint
A collection of scented plants must include mints. This
decorative form is the variegated apple mint, *Mentha
suaveolens* 'Variegata'. It has a running rootstock. Best
in shade. 60cm/2ft

Pelargonium tomentosum ◖ ●

Emerald velvet leaves smell of peppermint. Cut off the insignificant white flowers to encourage fresh foliage. Sprawling and tender. 1m/3ft

Pelargonium 'Mabel Grey' ○

One of the most strongly lemon-scented 'geraniums' with rough serrated leaves. Pinch out the flowers to encourage foliage. Tender. 1m/3ft

OTHER PLANTS WITH AROMATIC LEAVES INCLUDE:

Artemisia abrotanum
Eucalyptus p.88
Foeniculum vulgare (Fennel) p.189
Helichrysum angustifolium
Hyssopus officinalis (Hyssop) p.189
Laurus nobilis (Bay) p.210
Lavandula sp. (Lavender) p.207
Melissa officinalis 'Aurea' (Lemon balm) p.61
Monarda (Bergamot)
Origanum vulgare 'Aureum' (Oregano)
Ruta graveolens (Rue) p.71
Salvia officinalis (Sage)
Satureja montana (Winter savory)

Pelargonium 'Purple Unique' ○

A robust tender shrub which can be grown against a wall under glass. The lobed leaves have a musty smell. 1m/3ft+

Foliage Plants

The most successful gardens are those with a generous proportion of fine foliage plants (regardless whether they flower or not). Flowers are in bloom for only a relatively brief period, but graceful foliage will last for a minimum of six months and will prevent an area decaying into tat late in the season.

Of the groups below, use the grasses as quiet foils which will moderate strong hues in flowers, or plant them to act as a barrier between clashing neighbours. Also position them to make an arresting vertical contrast to plants with horizontally held leaves. Put the beautiful leafed plants beside subjects of coarser appearance to throw their own refinement into relief.

Plant the purple-leafed plants as a strong background contrast to pale companions such as the variegated-leafed plants which are the more curious for having plain neighbours. Or use the purple subjects to intensify a border composed of red flowers.

In addition to the plants on the following pages, it is worth considering the subjects listed in Architectural Plants on pages 52–9.

Helictotrichon sempervirens
(syn. *Avena candida*) (**Blue oat grass**) E:○
Neat, vivid blue-grey clumps with arching sprays of 'oats' in early summer. 45 × 30cm/ 1½ft × 1ft (1m/3ft in flower)

Carex comans (**bronze form**)
A stunning low-growing mophead sedge, the colouring of which is at its most intense in winter. Frost only serves to make it more beautiful. 60cm/2ft H and W

Spartina pectinata 'Aureomarginata'
A vigorous striking grass with yellow-striped leaves which appreciates moist soil where its rhizomes will spread indefinitely. Greenish flower-spikes with purple stamens in summer. 1.8m/6ft

Stipa gigantea E
Evergreen foliage with spraying appearance from which tall feathery buff plumes rise in summer. 75cm × 1m/2¹/₂ft × 3ft, and 1.8m/6ft high in flower

Miscanthus sinensis 'Silver Feather'
A very free-flowering form of a clump-forming grass which bears tall pale plumes of flowering spikes in autumn above the fountain of leaves.
1.8 × 1.2m/6 × 4ft

Stipa tenuissima ○
A shape of fountain-like grace and soft wispy seedheads in summer make this an attractive grass to include in a bed or border. 60 × 45cm/2 × 1¹/₂ft

Acer palmatum 'Dissectum'
A beautiful Japanese maple with very finely divided leaves, eventually forming an elegant mound. It turns a rich red in autumn. Can scorch in a hot position.
1 × 1.5m/3 × 5ft

Blechnum tabulare E: LH:
◑
This fern makes good running ground cover for moist neutral to acid soil. It is not fully hardy so requires a sheltered position. 60 × 45cm/ 2 × 1½ft

Eucalyptus gunnii E: ○
An Australian evergreen tree which, if kept pruned as a shrub, will continue to produce its small, round, blue juvenile leaves. Keep to 1.5m/5ft in height if used for foliage.

Artemisia 'Powis Castle'
Semi-E: ○
Exquisite silver-grey leaves of lacy texture on a cultivar which is the hardiest form of this shrub. Sun, shelter and good drainage are required. 75cm × 1m/ 2½ × 3ft

***Polystichum setiferum* Plumosodivisilobum ◑ ●**
This form of the soft shield fern has perhaps the most
glamorous of all leaves as they are softly textured and
very finely divided, spraying out to form a low mound.
45 × 60cm/1½ × 2ft

***Sambucus* 'Notcutt's Variety'**
A small shrub which is a filigree-leafed form of elder
and an effective and untricky substitute for the cut-
leafed *Acer palmatum* 'Dissectum'. 1m/3ft H and W

***Veratrum nigrum* ◑**
Large ribbed green leaves make a stunning and
majestic foliage plant with spikes of maroon flowers
on tall stems in late summer. (*V. album* has white
flowers.) A perennial for moist soil. 1.5m × 60cm/
5 × 2ft

Anthriscus sylvestris **'Ravenswing'**
Like a refined and beautiful cow parsley, this perennial makes an airy fountain of filigree leaves with umbels of white lace flowers in early summer. 1m × 60cm/3 × 2ft

Acer palmatum **'Dissectum Atropurpureum'**
Hummocky shrub with very finely cut purple-bronze leaves reddening in the autumn. This is the dark form of the plain green cultivar (*A.p. 'Dissectum'*) shown on page 88. 1 × 1.5m/3 × 5ft

Berberis thunbergii **'Rose Glow'**
Prettiest of the purple-leafed berberis with new growth on the shrub speckled with pale and deep pink before darkening. Bushy. 1.2m/4ft H and W

Cotinus coggygria **'Royal Purple' (Smoke tree)**
Very dark-foliaged shrub with feathery pink flowers in summer that resemble puffs of smoke. The leaves turn rich red in autumn. 4m/13ft H and W

CONSIDER ALSO:

Cordyline australis
'Atropurpurea' p.56
Malus × moerlandsii
'Profusion' p.238
Weigela florida 'Foliis
Purpureis' p.19

Heuchera 'Palace Purple'
Beautiful perennial with dark scalloped leaves and cream flower sprays in early summer. 45cm/1½ft H and W

Rosa glauca A shrub rose, and one of the most delicate subjects in this category, with mauve-grey leaves and, in midsummer, small pink, white-centred, single flowers followed by red fruits. 1.8 × 1.2m/ 6 × 4ft

Sedum maximum atropurpureum ○
Bronze-purple succulent leaves on red stems with a sadly drooping habit. Pale pink flower heads in late summer to autumn. 45 × 30cm/1½ × 1ft

Viola labradorica E
An invaluable spreading and self-seeding little plant (good everywhere except invading a precious rockery) with dark leaves and, in spring and early summer, pale violet scentless flowers. Happy in sun or shade. 15cm/6in H and W

Brunnera macrophylla 'Variegata' ◐
Eye-catching cream and green leaves (some almost entirely cream) on a herbaceous plant with blue flowers in spring.
45 × 30cm/1½ × 1ft

Aralia elata **'Variegata'**
Oustanding shrub or small tree with margined-white leaves and foaming sprays of white flowers in late summer. There is also a yellow-variegated form called 'Aureovariegata' of this Japanese angelica tree.
3.5 × 3m/12 × 10ft

Cornus alba **'Elegantissima'**
Useful shrub with white marked grey-green leaves. Suitable as a companion for neighbouring dark-leafed shrubs. 3m/10ft H and W

Consider also the
selection of variegated
shrubs shown in Gold
and Bright Green
Plants, pages 60–7.

Leucothöe fontanesiana **'Rainbow'** E: LH: ◑
Handsome evergreen shrub for acid soils with glossy,
purple-green leaves bearing pink, yellow and cream
variegation. Drooping sprays of white flowers in late
spring. 75cm × 1m/2¹/₂ × 3ft

Symphytum × uplandicum
'Variegatum'
This variegated comfrey
with its dazzling cream-
margined green leaves and
blue-mauve flowers in
high summer catches
attention. Cut out any
plain green leaves.
75 × 45cm/2¹/₂ × 1¹/₂ft

Weigela florida **'Variegata'** ○
An exceedingly pretty, bushy shrub the leaves of which
have fine cream margins. Soft pink flowers in early
summer when it is one of the most attractive plants in
the garden. 1.5m/5ft H and W

Paving Creepers

When a garden is laid with paving slabs, bricks, cobbles, gravels or any other type of hard material, it will look bleak unless this unrelieved ground surface is mellowed with small or prostrate plants. They are particularly useful for breaking up the rigid appearance of square or rectangular paving which is so often laid with monotonous regularity. A few of these little plants don't mind being walked on (especially thymes), but for the most part they are best inserted around the main areas of traffic. Their actual planting presents a problem if the masonry has been set in solid cement; in this case, all you can do is force out chunks of the mortar with a crowbar, replace it with earth and then insert the plants most tolerant of poor, arid conditions and keep them fed and watered until they have rooted down. The plants will have to be kept well watered until the roots have made a home for themselves.

***Armeria maritima* (Thrift)**
E: ○
Pin-cushion flowers in summer above vigorous, easy, spreading grassy mounds. There are white, pale pink and brick red forms too. 10 × 30cm/ 4in × 1ft

Androsace lanuginosa E or semi-E: ○
Beautiful mat-forming perennial with a trailing habit. Small heads of blush or lilac dark- or yellow-eyed flowers for a long period in summer. Happy on gravel. 5 × 30cm/2in × 1ft

Sagina subulata **'Aurea'** E: ○

A spreading mat of golden foliage completely spangled with minute white flowers in summer. For moist gritty soil. 2 × 30cm/1in × 1ft

Sedum spurium **'Dragon's Blood'** E: ○

Forms quick-growing carpets of green rosettes with rich red sprays of flowers in summer. 10 × 50cm/ 4in × 1 ft 8in. Nearly all sedums are ideal for hot, dry positions in full sun and for enlivening paving, paths, steps and walls.

Sempervivum arachnoideum **'Laggeri'** E: ○

One of the most delicately formed of the houseleeks, with silver cobwebs on its small rosettes and pink flowers in summer. 10 × 15cm/4 × 6in. Sempervivums endure hot, dry conditions and are ideal crevice fillers in sun.

Thymus serpyllum **'Coccineus'** E

Red flowers in summer above a carpet of tiny, scented leaves. Other excellent varieties for paving are 'Doone Valley' with gold-splashed foliage and *T. lanuginosus* with very woolly grey mats sprinkled with lilac-pink flowers in summer. 5 × 30cm+/2in × 1ft+

Trifolium repens **'Purpurascens'** (Purple-leafed clover) ○

Vigorous mat-forming purple variety of the common clover which will run between paving. It has white flowers in summer. 5 × 45cm/2in × 1¹/₂ft

Campanula cochleariifolia ○
A charming tiny bellflower with a running habit and massed stems of small blue, or slate or white flowers in summer. 5 × 60cm/2in × 2ft

Dianthus deltoides E: ○
The maiden pink forms a wide evergreen mat with crimson (or white or coral) flowers in summer. The white or blush-flowered *D. arenarius* with grassy grey leaves and *D. gratianopolitanus* shown on p. 116 are also ideal. 15 × 30cm/6in × 1ft

Campanula poscharskyana E
As vigorous as a weed, which is fine for paving cracks. Blue, starry flowers all summer and autumn in sun or shade above spreading mats. 12 × 60cm/5in × 2ft

***Helianthemum* 'Annabel'** E: ○
A lovely double form of the rock rose with grey-green leaves. Most varieties are single and the flowers don't last as long. A spreading drought-tolerant plant. 20 × 40cm/8in × 1ft 4in

Parahebe catarractae E: ○
Enthusiastic sub-shrub
massed with mauve, or in
another form, white,
flower-sprays zoned with
purple-red. For a
sheltered position as it is
not fully hardy.
30 × 45cm/1 × 1½ft

Phlox subulata **'Emerald Cushion'** E
Vigorous, mat-forming plant sheeted with flowers in
spring. White, pink, crimson, lavender and violet-
flowered cultivars are also obtainable. 10cm/4in H and
spread varies 20–45cm/8in–1½ft.

Saponaria ocymoides
Semi-E: ○
Very vigorous, spreading
or trailing mat of small
green leaves with showers
of pink flowers in summer.
15 × 60cm/6in × 2ft

Veronica prostrata (syn. *rupestris*) E
Very vigorous, spreading or trailing mat-forming plant
(ideal for steps) with rich blue flower spires in early
summer. 10 × 30cm/4in × 1ft

***Acaena* 'Blue Haze'** E
Very spreading, grey-leafed, red-stemmed plant for
poor, dry soils. 8cm/3½in. *A. adscendens* is an even more
rampant sprawler over paving. 12 × 90cm/5in × 3ft

***Antennaria dioica* 'Rosea'** E : ○
Another mat-former with fluffy pink flower-heads in
early summer and grey-green, silver-edged leaves.
12 × 60cm/5in × 2ft. *A. aprica* (syn. *parvifolia*) bears
white flowers.

***Cerastium tomentosum* 'Silver Carpet'** E
Small white flowers on thin stems in summer over grey-
leafed mats. Desperately invasive and needs confining or
can be used as a last resort where little else will grow or
is grown. 15cm/6in × indefinite spread

Tanacetum densum subsp. *amani* (syn. *Chrysanthemum haradjanii*) E: ○
Most beautiful mats of feathery, silver foliage. Small yellow flowers in summer. Not fully hardy.
10 × 45cm/4in × 1¹/₂ft

Othonna (syn. *Othonnopsis*) *cheirifolia* E: ○
Fleshy, grey, erectly held leaves on a plant with a trailing habit. Good for sunny steps. Yellow daisy flowers in summer. Not fully hardy. 30cm/1ft H and W

Veronica spicata subsp. *incana* Semi-E: ○
Spikes of sprawling bright blue flowers in summer appear above pointed leaves which are covered in silver hairs. 30cm/1ft H and W

Alpine and Dwarf Plants

Any gardener who wants to grow a large range of plants in a small space might consider specializing in alpines or dwarf plants. Conventionally these were grown in rock gardens, but the odd style of these gardens – the disruptive appearance of a group of rocks in otherwise flat surroundings – has encouraged other ways of growing alpines in recent decades. Raised beds or walls for trailing plants, or sinks and troughs for tiny subjects, or specially prepared peat beds for plants that are lime-intolerant are all attractive possibilities that are probably easier to accommodate in most gardens.

Alyssum spinosum roseum ○
A little spiny silver-green shrublet with clusters of pink flowers in summer forming a low mound. It is suited to a large trough, as shown. 20 × 30cm/ 8in × 1ft

***Campanula* 'Birch Hybrid'**
A showy vigorous spreader, good hanging over a wall, with open violet-blue bellflowers en masse in summer for a long period and small toothed leaves. 15 × 45cm/ 6in × 1½ft

Crassula sarcocaulis E, ○
A gnarled shrublet with spiky succulent leaves and starry
pink flowers, useful for their late-summer flowering.
Not fully hardy but is worth trying in a well-drained
sheltered spot. 20cm/8in H and W

**Dodecatheon meadia
(Shooting star)** ◑
Rich rose flowers with
prominent stamens bloom
on thin stems in spring
over rosettes of leathery
leaves. For moist soil.
25 × 15cm/10 × 6in

Dicentra cucullaria
A real charmer with milky, thickly textured flowers in
spring like little butterflies above glaucous ferny leaves.
It dies down soon after flowering. 15cm/6in H and W

Erodium guttatum ○
A small silver leafed perennial or sub-shrub which
bears distinctive flowers in summer, blush white with
two darkly blotched upper petals. 10 × 20cm/4 × 8in

Erodium 'Merstham Pink' ○
A very pretty form with pink flowers in summer. Like all erodiums it needs good drainage. 15 × 25cm/6 × 10in

Geranium cinereum var. subcaulescens 'Splendens' ○
A dazzling dwarf with dark-eyed flowers in summer. 10 × 25cm/4 × 10in

Euryops acraeus ○
A showy bushlet of sparkling silver-green leaves with massed golden daisies in early summer. Not fully hardy.
10 × 20cm/4 × 8in

Hebe 'Boughton Dome' E: ○
An evergreen shrub with the appearance of a conifer, this hebe is grown for its smoothly rounded formation. Slow growing. 45cm/1½ft H and W, though eventually larger.

Hypericum olympicum ○
A neat bush with grey-green leaves and golden flowers in early summer. Needs good drainage. 20 × 25cm/8 × 10in

Moltkia suffruticosa ○
A little sub-shrub with nodding heads of rich blue flowers in early summer and dark green leaves.
25 × 30cm/10in × 1ft

Picea abies **'Gregoryana'**
E: O
A tiny domed conifer, small enough to include in a trough or sink. 30cm/1ft H and W

Sedum spathulifolium **'Cape Blanco'** E: ○
A dazzling sedum forming rosettes of silver leaves which are covered with yolk-yellow starry flowers in summer.
7.5 × 20cm/3 × 8in

Veronica pinnata **'Blue Eyes'**
Enjoying a leafier soil than most alpines, it sends up spires of small, intensely blue flowers in spring and early summer.
10 × 30cm/4in × 1ft

CONSIDER ALSO:

Androsace lanuginosa p.94
Antennaria dioica 'Rosea' p.98
Aubrieta deltoidea p.31
Campanula garganica p.31
Cassiope 'Muirhead' p.36
Cyclamen coum p.136
Dianthus 'Pike's Pink' p.32
Daphne cneorum 'Eximia' p.15
Euphorbia myrsinites p.33
Gentiana sino-ornata p.40
Lewisia cotyledon p.41
Phlox adsurgens 'Wagon Wheel' p.41
Phlox 'Emerald Cushion' p.97
Rhodohypoxis baurii p.42
Sempervivum p.117
Tanacetum densum subsp. *amani* p.99

Ground-cover Plants

Ground-cover plants, whether shrubs or perennials, are subjects whose habit of dense growth suppresses the weeds which might grow beneath them. If you confine your plantings to weed-suppressors only, you will achieve the kind of garden that is nearly labour-free.

Almost any plant whose skirt comes right down to the ground and is evergreen (or, if herbaceous or deciduous, is nonetheless densely leafy) qualifies as a weed-suppressor. So a large number of other plants mentioned elsewhere in this book will fulfil this role and you can use these to supplement the list below of effective shrubs and perennials. However, in all cases, the ground has to be kept weed-free until the plants establish themselves, join up and take over the job themselves. After this stage your only task will be to curb by cutting back (or digging up) the more vigorous plants which threaten to ramp outside their territory.

Cornus canadensis (Creeping dogwood) LH
Plant for sun or shade but needs peaty, lime-free soil. Creamy-white flower bracts in early summer followed by clustered red berries. 15 × 60cm/ 6in × 2ft

Dicentra 'Bacchanal' ◑ ●
Very accommodating running herbaceous plant with bright green leaves and pendent crimson flowers in spring to summer for a long period. 45cm/1¹/₂ft H and W

Ajuga reptans 'Pink Surprise' E
Neat carpeter with bright pink flower spikes in late spring and bronze leaves. 15 × 60cm/6in × 2ft. There are also several other cultivars, the best of which is 'Burgundy Glow'. 10 × 45cm/4in × 1¹/₂ft

Epimedium E: ◑ in variety
All excellent for cool, shady positions. *E. youngianum* has white flowers in the form 'Niveum' (shown above), *E. grandiflorum* 'Rose Queen' is pink, both blooming in late spring. Other epimediums bear similarly shaped flowers in yellow, orange, red or mauve. One of the most vigorous is the yellow *E. perralderianum*. 30cm/1ft H and W

Geranium in some variety
G. endressii is one of the best, a colonizer in sun or shade, bearing a perpetual succession of pink flowers. 45 × 60cm/1½ × 2ft. Other good varieties include *G.* 'Johnson's Blue' (shown on p. 162) and *G. macrorrhizum* (shown on p. 174)

CONSIDER ALSO:

Alchemilla mollis p.52
Bergenia p.52
Hellebores in variety
Hosta in variety

***Persicaria bistorta* 'Superba'**
Vigorous and even rampant in moist soil with pink poker flower spikes in summer and sometimes autumn also, over light green leaves. 1m × 60cm/3 × 2ft

***Rodgersia pinnata* 'Superba' ◐**
A most beautiful foliage plant for moist even boggy soils. This has pink fluffy flowers in summer over leaves which resemble those of a horse chestnut. Almost all rodgersias make good ground-cover. 1m/3ft H and W

***Tellima grandiflora* E: ◐ ●**
Clump-forming plant with hairy, scalloped leaves and spires of cream and green bell-flowers in late spring. The form 'Purpurea' has bronze leaves. 60 × 30cm/ 2 × 1ft

Ceratostigma
plumbaginoides ○
A running sub-shrub with
a succession of bright blue
flowers in autumn when
the leaves colour hotly.
15 × 60cm/6in × 2ft

Cotoneaster dammeri E: ◑
A dense ground hugging evergreen mat with red fruits
in autumn, following minute white flowers in spring.
30cm × 3m/1ft × 10ft

Cytisus × ***kewensis*** ○
Prostrate and spreading broom which is laden with
sprays of creamy-yellow flowers in late spring. Its
arching habit makes it suitable for covering a bank.
25cm × 1m/10in × 3ft

Heathers in variety; E: most LH.
The dwarf *Erica* and *Calluna* are amongst the most commonly planted groups for ground cover. *Erica carnea* (shown above) with red, white or pink flowers and green or golden foliage is lime-tolerant. Winter/spring flowers. 30 × 45cm/1 × 1½ft

Erica × darleyensis is also lime-tolerant. It flowers in winter to early spring. 45cm × 1m/1½ × 3ft.

Hebe in some variety: E.
H. rakaiensis (syn. *subalpina*) is one of the best for this purpose, forming a small-leafed, evergreen, apple-green hummock with small white flowers in summer. 75cm × 1m/2½ × 3ft

Juniperus horizontalis **'Wiltonii' ('Blue rug')** ○
There are many ground-hugging junipers, all enjoying
sun and good drainage. The whipcord foliage of this
variety can become tinged with purple in winter.
30cm × 1.8m/1 × 6ft

Hypericum calycinum
(Rose of Sharon) E or
Semi-E
This is an invasive shrub
(occasionally subject to
rust) so is best confined to
those areas such as slopes
where few other plants will
cope. 30cm × 1.5m/
1 × 5ft

Juniperus sabina tamariscifolia E: ○
Very spreading conifer forming a flat top; foliage is grey
when young but a rich green later. 1m × 2m/3 × 6½ft.
See also *J.* 'Pfitzeriana Aurea' on p. 49.

Gaultheria (syn. *Pernettya*)
mucronata E: LH: ◑
Showy evergreen for acid
soils, forming dense
suckering thickets. Small
white heath-like flowers in
spring followed by clusters
of berries from white to
pink or cherry-red. Plant
in groups to ensure
fruiting. 75cm × 1.2m/
2½ × 4ft

***Lithodora diffusa* 'Heavenly Blue'** E: LH: ○
A large, small-leafed mat covered with bright blue
flowers over a long period from late spring onwards.
Needs good drainage and lime-free soil.
7.5cm × 60cm/3in × 2ft

***Sarcococca hookeriana* var.
*digyna*** E: ◑
Suckering shrub with
glossy dark green leaves.
Useful for shade and for
the intensely fragrant but
insignificant flowers in late
winter. 75cm × 1m/2½ × 3ft

Viburnum davidii E: ◑
Shrub of fine architectural form making a mound of
glossy, dark green leaves. Turquoise-blue, egg-shaped
fruits in autumn (following small white flowers in
summer) if a small group are planted together to
ensure cross-pollination. 1 × 1.5m/3 × 5ft

Plants for Difficult Spots

All gardens have troublesome areas where few plants will thrive, and these problems tend to occur in concentrated numbers near the house. The difficulty may be darkness caused by neighbouring buildings which block out the light, or it might be the sort of dry shade cast by a tree. Dankness as well as darkness is possible, perhaps in a gloomy corner where the house guttering drips. The converse of this type of problem is equally challenging where, for example, a terrace is simply an unshaded stone waste which cooks in summer. And arguably the worst problem of all is caused by a burial mound of rubble and hardcore which has been used in the construction of house or terrace. This proves to be usually a tomb for plants as well.

Short of drastic overhaul, the most sensible way of dealing with such problem areas is to place here only those plants which will endure these particular conditions. More vulnerable plants will be doomed.

Ferns are invaluable here, like the evergreen hart's tongue fern (*Asplenium scolopendrium*) with shining green fronds. It has crested variants.
40 × 30cm/1ft 4in × 1ft

***Gentiana asclepiadea* (Willow gentian)**
Graceful plant with Oxford blue (or white in the form 'Alba') tubular flowers in late summer–early autumn. It requires peaty soil. 60 × 30cm/2 × 1ft

Omphalodes cappadocica
A quickly running plant with bright blue small flowers in spring. 15 × 30cm/ 6in × 1ft

***Primula vulgaris* (Primrose)**
The common primrose produces a
succession of pale lemon flowers in early
spring. 7.5 × 15cm/3 × 6in

***Smilacina racemosa* LH**
Sprays of creamy flowers in spring over
arching foliage. This elegant perennial
needs moist leafy soil. 75 × 45cm/2½ ×
1½ft

CONSIDER ALSO:

Ajuga p.104
Astilbe p.161
Astrantia carniolica
  p.161
Epimedium p.104
Heuchera p.175
Hosta in variety
Milium effusum
  'Aureum' p.61
Primula japonica
P. pulverulenta p.186
Pulmonaria p.137
Tellima grandiflora
  p.105
Tiarella cordifolia
Viola in variety

Vinca (Periwinkle) E
These sub-shrubs make spring-flowering ground-cover,
suited to banks. *V. major* (45cm/1½ft H and W) is the
rampant form. *V. minor* (22 × 30cm/9in × 1ft) has smaller
leaves. Both have variegated forms. Spring flowers of
blue, white or garnet.

Euphorbia cyparissias
Stems with grey-green leaves look like squirrels' tails.
Lime-yellow flower-heads in early summer, on a running
plant that makes invasive but good ground-cover.
25 × 30cm+/10in × 1ft+

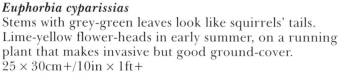

Digitalis purpurea E
The Excelsior foxglove has
most impact with 1.5m/5ft
spikes; flowers of white,
pink, apricot, primrose or
purple. *D. lutea* is shorter
with yellow flowers. *D.* ×
mertonensis is purplish
pink; 75cm/2½ft. Summer-
blooming, short-lived
perennials or biennials for
light soil. × 30cm/1ft

Epimedium × ***perralchicum*** E
A ground-cover plant with glossy green leaves and
sprays of spurred yellow flowers in spring. 45cm/1½ft
H and W

***Helleborus foetidus* (Stinking hellebore)**
Dark green fingered leaves with maroon-rimmed ice-
green flower bells opening in early spring and lasting
for a long period. 45cm/1¹/₂ft H and W

***Iris foetidissima* (Gladwin
iris)** E
Broad leaves and quiet
lilac or yellow flowers in
summer, showy orange-
scarlet seed-pods in
autumn. 45cm/1¹/₂ft
H and W

***Lamium galeobdolon* 'Florentinum'** (syn. 'Variegatum') E
A ground-coverer of the nettle family. Silver and dark
green foliage; pale yellow flowers in early summer.
Rampant. 30cm/1ft × indefinite

CONSIDER ALSO:

Alchemilla mollis p.52
Asperula odorata
Bergenia p.52
Euphorbia robbiae p.215
Millium effusum
  'Aureum' p.61
Polygonatum × hybridum
  p.219
Tellima grandiflora
  p.105
Tiarella cordifolia
Viola labradorica p.91

CONSIDER ALSO:

Acanthus spinosus p.54
Allium in variety
Armeria p.94
Anthemis cupaniana
   p.214
Cerastium p.98
Cynara p.56
Eryngium in variety
Festuca glauca p.69
Foeniculum p.189
Gypsophila p.34
Linum in variety
Onopordum p.57
Othonna cheirifolia p.99
Phlomis fruticosa
Sisyrinchium striatum
   p.165
Thyme p.95
Verbascum
Yucca p.57
Also all plants on pp.
   68–73 (Grey and
   Silver Plants) which
   are distinguished by
   the sign ○.

***Cistus × pulverulentus
'Sunset'* (Sun rose)** E: ○
Compact shrub with grey-green leaves and magenta flowers produced prolifically in summer. Not fully hardy. 1m/3ft H and W. All other cistus are also suited to this position.

***Helianthemum* 'Wisley
Primrose'** (Sun rose) E: O
Lemon yellow flowers over grey-green leaves on this single-flowered form. The individual flowers are fleeting but there is a prolonged display. All helianthemums are likewise suited to this position. 25 × 45cm/ 10in × 1½ft

Iris germanica ○
The bearded iris needs its rhizomes baked by sun. The colour range includes white, green, yellow, bronze, pink, carmine, wine, pale to deep blue, lavender to purple as well as bicolours. 60cm–1.2m × 30cm/2–4 × 1ft

***Rosmarinus* (Rosemary)** E: ○

The aromatic, grey-green leafed shrub, for culinary as well as ornamental use. Small blue flowers in spring, at their brightest in the shrub 'Severn Sea'. There is also an erect-growing form called 'Fastigiatus' or 'Miss Jessop's Variety'. The ordinary rosemary (*Rosmarinus officinalis*) reaches about 1.2 × 1m/ 4 × 3ft.

Senecio leucostachys E: ○
Filigree, silvery white leaves on stems which intermesh with shrubs or a wall trellis. Small white flowers in summer. Tender. 60cm (more in mild winter areas) × 45cm/2 × 1½ft

***Salvia officinalis* (Sage)** E: ○
The best foliage forms of this shrubby sage are the purple-leafed 'Purpurascens', shown above, the variegated green and gold 'Icterina', and 'Tricolor' with its grey-green leaves marked with white, pink and purple. Spikes of blue-purple flowers in summer.

Dutch iris
A hybrid of *I. xiphium* and related species, the Dutch iris provides an easy, glamorous show in early summer. The colour range includes blue and gold. 60 × 10cm/2ft × 4in

Dianthus gratianopolitanus E: ○
The Cheddar pink with its pink flowers and cushion of
leaves is easy and usually naturalizes. It bears very
fragrant blooms in midsummer. 15cm/6in H and W

Centranthus ruber (**Valerian**)
Maroon, rose or white flower-sprays on a plant which
often naturalizes in walls. Self-sowing and invasive. A
beautiful plant but its seed-heads need to be cut off if
it is to be controlled.
60 × 45cm/2 × 1½ft

Mesembryanthemum (**Livingstone daisy**) E: ○
A large family of mostly trailing succulents with rayed
flowers blooming all summer in a brilliant colour range.
They need sun to thrive and complete winter cover as
all are tender. 15 × 30cm/6in × 1ft

Nasturtium (*Tropaeolum majus*) ○
Frost-tender, but will flower summer through till late
autumn on gritty soil if it is not too poor. It is obtainable
in shades of red, yellow or orange, and with plain green
or marbled green and cream leaves. Single or double
flowers. 15 × 45cm/6in × 1¹/₂ft

Sempervivum **'Commander
Hay'** E: ○
A cultivar with large rosy
rosettes and pink flowers
in summer. 20cm/8in H
and W. Almost all the
houseleek varieties will
adapt to these conditions.

Sedum album tenuifolium murale **(Wall sedum)** E: ○
Invasively self-sowing though useful in the right
position, this little white flowered succulent will spill
down steps or in paving. 10 × 15cm/4 × 6in

The Four Seasons

The best gardens remain beautiful at all seasons. Not an easy requirement, so it has to be planned. As each new season replaces the last, the appearance of the garden changes and gives a succession of new pleasures. Glistening berries follow flowers, autumn blossom takes over from summer which has succeeded spring. And in a well-planned garden, even winter brings its choice flowers, scents and fruits.

Shrubs for Seasonal Display

Whether you are planting a mixed or a shrub border, it is a good idea to ensure some continuity of flowering throughout the year. A selection of flowers for winter is given on pages 138–9 but here is a choice of some of the best flowering shrubs for a spring to autumn display. They represent a possible nucleus to which you can add shrubs from the rest of the book.

You might decide to confine yourself to different representatives of just one (or two) genus for a particular season. If so, arguably the best for spring are camellias; for midsummer and after, roses (with cistus quite a good second in mild-winter areas, even though they are not reliably hardy nor as long-lived); for later summer and into autumn, hydrangeas. These groups alone will given you an enormous choice of cultivars.

Berberis darwinii E
Clustered orange flowers followed by dusky blue fruits on a large, prickly weed-suppressing shrub, growing to 4m/13ft H and W.

Forsythia × intermedia
A vigorous shrub which makes a very showy display early in the year, which makes up for its rather dull green foliage. One of the best cultivars is 'Lynwood'. 3 × 1.8m/ 10 × 6ft

Camellia × williamsii 'Galaxie' E: LH: ◑
This bushy shrub with glossy dark green leaves is arguably one of the most floriferous of all the camellias. It makes twiggy growth which is festooned with masses of soft pink flowers, veined with a deeper rose. It is a manageable choice for a small garden. 1.5 × 1.2m/5 × 4ft

Magnolia liliiflora 'Nigra'
LH: ○
Dark wine-red flowers like
huge elongated tulips
bloom from mid-spring to
midsummer and
sometimes recurrently
later. It forms a compact
hardy shrub of 4 × 3m/
13 × 10ft.

Magnolia stellata (Star magnolia)
White many-petalled starry flowers cover the shrub in
early spring. It is not vigorous but a valuable lime-
tolerant magnolia. 3 × 4m/10 × 13ft

**_Spiraea × arguta_ (Bridal
veil)**
The most elegant of the
spiraeas with arching
growth, festooned with
white flowers. 2.4m/8ft H
and W

Viburnum × juddii
Very sweetly scented flowers
which are pink in bud, white
when open, bloom freely
from mid to late spring.
1.5m/5ft H and W

Rhododendron 'Golden Torch' E: LH: ◑
This Yakushimanum hybrid makes a
dome-forming evergreen shrub which is
covered in soft pinky-cream clusters of
open flowers in mid-spring. 1m/
3ft H and W

Rhododendron 'Praecox' Semi-E: LH: ◑
This shrub blooms very early in spring
when its delicate rosy-purple flowers are
freely produced. 1.2 × 1m/4 × 3ft

CONSIDER ALSO:
Ceanothus (spring-
flowering forms in
variety)
Magnolia × soulangeana

***Cistus × cyprius* (Sun rose)** E: ○
A good example of a group of beautiful
but often slightly tender shrubs, all
requiring full sun, light soil and no
manure. This is one of the hardiest with
white flowers with a deep maroon central
blotch and leaden green leaves.
1.8 × 1.2m/6 × 4ft

Cistus × purpureus E: ○
This sun rose is not fully hardy but worth
growing in a sheltered position for its
long, magnificent display of deep rose
flowers with maroon blotches and soft
grey-green foliage. Bushy growth to
1.5 × 1.8m/5 × 6ft

CONSIDER ALSO:

Carpenteria californica
   p.50
Cistus 'Peggy Sammons'
   p.51
Cistus × pulverulentus
Paeonia delavayi p.29
P.d. var. *ludlowii* p.181
Roses on pages 78–9,
   224–5

***Paeonia suffruticosa* (Tree peony)** ○
A glorious shrub of which there are many named forms.
This is 'Sitifukujin', a Japanese cultivar, with huge
golden-bossed rose blooms and glaucous foliage. Shade
from morning sun. 1.2 × 1.5m/4 × 5ft

Rose ○

A vast genus, but the most useful roses for the border are either the repeat-flowering shrub roses, or reasonably disease-resistant cultivars of the floribunda roses, or else a selected few of those roses that supply a fine display of autumn fruit after blooming. Of the first group we show here an old Hybrid Musk shrub rose, 'Cornelia' with clusters of small, pink, salmon-flushed flowers from early summer to autumn. 1.8 × 2.1m/6 × 7ft

The fruiting category of roses is represented here by 'Frau Dagmar Hastrup', a healthy Rugosa rose with large, single pink flowers from early to late summer, followed by crimson heps. 1.5m/5ft H and W

'Golden Wings' is one of the most elegant of the modern shrub roses, a large single yellow in continuous bloom, growing to 1.2m/4ft H and W.

Floribunda or cluster-flowered roses produce their blooms almost continuously from summer to autumn. 'Amber Queen' is a very fragrant example with neat bushy growth. 60cm/2ft H and W

Hydrangea 'Blue Wave' ◖
One of a group of hardy
shrubs making a fine
display in summer to mid-
autumn. This form is a
vigorous lace-cap growing
to 1.8 × 2.1m/6 × 7ft.
Lime-free soil is necessary
to ensure blue flowers;
slightly limy soil will
produce pink or red
flowers; very alkaline soils
are unsuitable.

Deutzia setchuenensis corymbiflora
Most of the deutzias are pretty, early-summer-flowering
shrubs, but this is arguably the most elegant and more
valuable for its blooms in the second half of the summer.
Starry white flowers in corymbs. Not fully hardy.
1.5 × 1m/5 × 3ft

Fuchsia **'Margaret'**
Fuchsias bloom
continuously from summer
until frosts. This is a
vigorous bushy form with
rich deep pink sepals and
a violet corolla. It is not
fully hardy. Don't cut off
the top growth, which may
have died in the winter,
until the spring. 1.4 × 1m/
4 × 3ft

CONSIDER ALSO:

Buddleja davidii p.180
Fuchsias in variety
Hebe in variety on page
   107
Hydrangea villosa

Hydrangea paniculata
A lovely shrub flowering from late
summer to early autumn with long
panicles of fertile and sterile florets. In
the form 'Grandiflora' the inflorescence is
up to 30cm/1ft long. For moist rich soil.
2.7 × 2.1m/9 × 7ft

Hydrangea quercifolia (**Oak-leafed
hydrangea**) ◖
This variety has pendent, cream, lacy
panicles in midsummer to autumn. Its
bold foliage, cut like that of an oak, often
colours richly in autumn. 1.5 × 2.1m/
5 × 7ft

Acer palmatum 'Atropurpureum'
A Japanese maple with finely cut bronzy purple foliage
which turns brilliant red in the autumn. It needs
protection from strong sun and cold winds. 4.5m/15ft
H and W

Fothergilla major LH
White, bottle-brush flower-spikes in spring, and flame
and yellow autumn foliage make this a dual-season
shrub. Peaty, lime-free soil. 3m/10ft H and W

Enkianthus campanulatus
LH: ◐
Pale buff, pendent bell-
flowers in clusters in early
summer, a tiered-branch
habit and rich autumn
foliage. Peaty, lime-free
soil, part-shade. 3m/10ft H
and W

Euonymus alatus
This is a slow-growing
shrub with a spreading
habit. The leaves turn a rich
and deepening red in the
autumn. 3/10ft H and W

Rhus typhina 'Laciniata'
(syn. 'Dissecta') ○
The cut-leafed female
cultivar of the popular
stag's-horn sumach
provides rich autumn
colour. Conical fruits
persisting in winter.
2.7 × 4.5m/9 × 15ft

Callicarpa bodinieri var. ***geraldii*** ○
A shrub that produces extraordinary small violet
berries in the autumn when the foliage also turns
mauve. Plant several bushes together to ensure
satisfactory pollination. 2.1 × 1.8m/7 × 6ft

Cornus kousa var. ***chinensis*** (**Chinese dogwood**)
A shrub with a dual display of wonderful white 'flowers'
(bracts) in summer followed by strawberry-like fruits.
3.6 × 4m/12 × 13ft

Cotoneaster salicifolius '**Exburyensis**' E
An arching graceful hybrid shrub with bunches of small
yellow fruits in autumn that persist on the branches.
5m/16ft H and W

Rosa moyesii 'Geranium'
Single scarlet flowers in early summer followed by large, red, bottle-shaped autumn fruits. Bushy, erect growth.
2.4 × 2.1m/8 × 7ft

Viburnum opulus 'Xanthocarpum'
A vigorous and healthy form of the guelder rose with golden translucent berries in autumn following on from the white lace-cap flowers.
4m/13ft H and W

Skimmia japonica E: ◑
The females berry if pollinated by a male. The best combination is the female cultivar 'Foremanii' which produces abundant berries, planted with the male 'Fragrans' with its scented, creamy flower spikes in early summer. Both are evergreen and better in part-shade.
1 × 1.5m/3 × 5ft

CONSIDER ALSO:

Arbutus unedo p.244
Cotoneaster frigidus 'Cornubia' p.244
Malus 'Evereste' p.244
Pernettya (Gaultheria) mucronata p.109
Pyracantha in variety p.198

Bulbs, Corms etc through the Year

Bulbs are the ideal subject for a small area, because they will give colour in the minimum space and in return for minimum effort. Also they can be chosen to give flowers each month of the year, even in winter when little else is in bloom. Plant them where they will suffer the least disturbance. Strong-growing bulbs are suitable between herbaceous plants and deciduous shrubs, even at the foot of deciduous trees if they do not demand a sunny, open position. Small, choice and difficult bulbs will probably need planting in a separate area, lest they are swamped by their ranker neighbours. Tender subjects which require a summer baking can be placed at the foot of sunny walls where they can act as a sumptuous carpet for climbers. Stiff, upright bulbs like hybrid tulips which need to be lifted each year are suited to formal open-ground displays. Species bulbs which will naturalize are most appealing when scattered in groups of informal appearance.

Anemone nemorosa ◗
A single, white or lilac-flushed flower in the wild form, good for naturalizing; though near a house, the double white form (shown here) or one of the single pale blue cultivars or lavender 'Allenii' is more suitable. 15cm/6in

Anemone blanda
This wind flower is sun-loving and spreading on light soil; white, blue, pink or deep rose in the form 'Radar'. It is fully hardy but as it blooms at a chilly time of the year, will benefit from a sheltered spot. 8cm/3in

Chionodoxa luciliae
Blue (or pink or white)
stars on a bulb spreading
invasively in light soil,
forming mass colour.
8cm/3in

***Erythronium* 'White Beauty' ◑**
Exquisite bulb for cool leafy soil which does not dry out.
25cm/10in. Other fine hybrids include the lemon
'Kondo' and yellow 'Pagoda' both with marbled leaves.

***Fritillaria meleagris* 'Aphrodite'**
White form of the snake's head fritillary, the type
plant bearing bells with a plum-red chequer pattern,
also shown. For moist soil, sun or light shade.
25cm/10in

Fritillaria imperialis
The yellow or rusty-red crown imperial needs sun and
well-drained soil; it has a pungent smell and is one of
the most distinctive bulbs one can grow. In heavy soils
the bulb can be planted slightly on its side, or sand/grit
added to the earth. 1m/3ft

For further tulips see
page 211.

Narcissus **'Thalia'**
This is one of the best white trumpet daffodils
(30cm/1ft) though the slightly larger 'Mount Hood'
surpasses it for naturalizing.

Leucojum aestivum
Flourishing in moist soil,
'Gravetye Giant' is the
finest form of the
snowflake. Up to 60cm/2ft

Tulipa kaufmanniana
'Gaiety' ○
A vigorous cultivar which
flowers in early spring.
20cm/8in

Tulips ○
Of the numerous hybrids, 'Burgundy' is one of the
richest coloured of the lily-flowering cultivars, which
are fairly resistant to bad weather. All this group have
flowers of elegant form. 45cm/1½ft

CONSIDER ALSO:

Crocosmia in variety
Zantedeschia aethiopica
'Crowborough' p.187

Allium aflatunense ○
A handsome ornamental onion flowering in early summer. There is also a darker striking variant called 'Purple Sensation'. 75cm/2½ft

Allium christophii ○
One of the most dazzling onions with huge starry lilac heads on a 40cm/1ft 4in stem in summer. Good for drying. The handsome architecturally formed heads and stems will last for years when dried.

Camassia leichtlinii
Easy in heavy, rather moist soils, with white or blue flowers. The plants have untidy leaves which die down soon after flowering. 75cm+/2½ft+

Galtonia candicans ○
Strap-like leaves and ivory, sometimes green-tipped bells on 1m/3ft stems (seen here in front of grey-stemmed verbascums). For well drained but moist soil.

Gladiolus × colvillei (syn *nanus*) ○
Delicately pretty and long-flowering, peach-pink, white or orange cultivars, with contrastingly pale and dark throats. For light soil; not always hardy.
30–45cm/1–1½ft

Lilium candidum ○
The fragrant madonna lily, needing sun, a heavy soil and no disturbance. The basal leaves appear in autumn and persist through the winter. 1.2m/4ft

Lilium martagon ◑
With pink-purple or white flowers for semi-shade and leafy soil where it will naturalize.
60cm–1.2m/2–4ft

Lilium 'Stargazer' ○
A magnificent and fragrant lily which is suitable for a pot or in the garden. The flowers open on 1m/3ft stems. It is a very showy cultivar and a good garden plant.

Crinum × powellii ○
Magnificent pale to deep
pink or white flowers on a
tall stem above spreading
strap-shaped leaves. In
cold areas, will do best at
the foot of a hot wall
where it may need
watering to induce free-
flowering. Protect in harsh
winters. 1m/3ft

***Colchicum autumnale* (Autumn crocus)**
There are white forms of this bulb, and also double as
well as single, but all bloom in autumn when the plant is
leafless. The following spring a sheaf of large leaves
appears before dying away. Up to 15cm/6in

Schizostylis 'Sunrise' ○
A good pink form of the
Kaffir lily. *S. coccinea* is
crimson red. They need
full sun and well-drained
though not dry soil. Not
fully hardy. 60cm/2ft

Nerine bowdenii ○
Valuable bulb for its late, glistening pink flowers, freely
produced. 'Fenwick's Variety' is slightly taller with larger
flowers. For well-drained soil. Not fully hardy.
45–60cm/1¹/₂–2ft

Crocus in variety
C. tommasinianus, lavender in the type, though shown here in its deep form, 'Whitewell Purple' is a pretty though sometimes invasively self-sowing variety for winter or earliest spring. *C. chrysanthus*, especially in its rich blue forms like 'Bluebird', 'Blue Pearl' or 'Zenith' is also beautiful. 7.5cm/3in

Cyclamen hederifolium (syn. *C. neapolitanum*) ◗
This pretty cyclamen produces its rose or white flowers in autumn above silver-marbled leaves. It will self-sow and gradually produce a carpet of blossom. 7.5cm/3in

Eranthis hyemalis
Where happy, the winter aconite will spread into a carpet of bright gold, green-ruffed flowers. 7.5cm/3in

CONSIDER ALSO:

Winter-flowering
  bulbs, p. 136
Bulbs for the foot of
  hedges, pp. 210–11

Galanthus nivalis
The snowdrop has many variants, including double forms but the ordinary single type is the best for naturalizing. 10cm/4in

Iris unguicularis (syn. *I. stylosa*) E: ○
A winter-flowering rhizomatous perennial available in white or lavender forms of which 'Mary Barnard' is the deepest colour. Good drainage is necessary. 30cm/1ft

Winter Flowers

A problem common to all gardens in cold climates is how to keep them attractive and inviting throughout winter. One solution is to include a high proportion of evergreens amongst the plants. The other answer is to establish a fair number of winter-flowering subjects. Admittedly the amount of plants that bloom reliably in winter is minuscule compared with their spring and summer counterparts, but the actual range is nonetheless wide and includes bulbs, herbaceous plants, small and large shrubs. Plant the small subjects in strong clusters, spaced at intervals so that their presence can be seen at a distance and so that they enliven a greater area of the garden.

Supplement the list below with the winter flowering bulbs on page 135, the brightly-coloured evergreens on pages 60–7, and some of the bolder-leafed evergreens on pages 52–9.

Cyclamen coum ◑
This small bulb flowers in winter or earliest spring. There are white or magenta forms, both with plain dark green leaves. 7.5cm/3in

Iris reticulata '**Harmony**' ○
This kind of iris will give a dependable annual show in late winter/early spring if the bulb is planted in moist but well drained conditions. 10cm/4in

Narcissus bulbocodium ○
The yellow hoop-petticoat narcissi are spring charmers, one of the earliest and best being the soft lemon *N.b. romieuxii* in mid-winter. Good drainage is essential. 12.5cm/5in

Narcissus cyclamineus
Charming small daffodil
with a long trumpet and
completely swept-back
petals in early spring. For
acid soils. 15cm/6in

Scilla mischtschenkoana (syn. *tubergeniana*) ◐
In very early spring, each bulb produces about three
flower spikes, the silver blue petals marked with darker
blue veins. A good naturalizer. 10cm/4in

Viola odorata E
The sweet violet can be in
bloom from February on.
Wine-red, white, pink and
yellow cultivars as well as
violet. Its green leaves
form a spreading carpet.
10 × 30cm/4in × 1ft

Helleborus orientalis E: ◐
The most invaluable of all late winter/early spring
flowers. A huge range of shades is obtainable from white
to deepest black, all with handsome divided foliage.
Other valuable hellebores include *H. foetidus* (p.113) and
H. argutifolius (p.53). 30–45 × 45cm/1–1¹/₂ × 1¹/₂ft

***Pulmonaria* (Lungwort)** ◐
The earliest to bloom is *P. rubra* in late winter with
plain green leaves and coral-red flowers, followed by
a succession of different lungworts. 'Sissinghurst
White', above, is a particularly pretty one for early
spring. All 15–30 × 30cm/6in–1ft × 1ft

***Chimonanthus praecox
(Winter Sweet)*** ○
Very fragrant pale yellow
flowers, stained purple,
rather larger in the
cultivar 'Grandiflorus'.
Give it a sunny wall.
2.5m/8ft H and W

Clematis cirrhosa var.
balearica E:○
Give this climber a
sheltered wall for its
flowers which appear from
mid-winter onwards.
Finely-cut leaves and pale
green, nodding blooms
with red spots within. Up
to 4m/13ft

***Camellia* 'Nobilissima'** E: LH: ◑
One of the earliest of the *C. japonica*
hybrids with large snowy blossoms in late
winter/early spring. These turn buff
before falling. *C. sasanqua* 'Narumigata' is
a true winter flowerer, opening its white
flowers from carmine buds in early winter
but it is not fully hardy. Both are best on
a wall that avoids early sun which will
blight the flowers if they are frosted.
3m/10ft H and W

Corylopsis pauciflora LH:
◑
Small fragrant pale yellow
bells hang along the
branches in early spring of
this bushy shrub. The
leaves are bronze when
first emerging before
greening. 1.5m/5ft
H and W

Daphne mezereum ○
Scented reddish purple
flowers (or white in the
variety 'Alba') cluster along
the stems in late winter or
earliest spring. 1m/3ft
H and W

***Daphne odora
'Aureomarginata'*** E: ○
A shapely bush which
needs a sunny sheltered
position, with cream-
bordered evergreen leaves
and intensely fragrant
flowers in small clusters in
earliest spring. 1 × 1.5m/
3 × 5ft

Jasminum nudiflorum
A shrub best trained on a wall to control its long, green, trailing stems. Wonderful show of yellow flowers throughout late autumn to early spring. 3m/10ft H and W

CONSIDER ALSO:

Erica × darleyensis p.107
Viburnum × bodnantense 'Dawn', p.77

Hamamelis × intermedia **'Pallida'** LH
One of the loveliest Chinese witch-hazels with spreading branches massed in late winter onwards with pale yellow flowers. Bold leaves. 4m/13ft H and W

Rhododendron **'Bric-a-Brac'** E: LH: ◐
A lovely and floriferous hybrid which flowers in late winter to early spring. Its flowers are vulnerable to frosts and it benefits from a sheltered position. For moist woodland soil. 1.5m/5ft H and W

Rhododendron moupinense E: LH: ◐
Species with white, pale or dark pink flowers (sometimes freckled) blooming in late winter/early spring. It needs peaty soil and part shade. 1m/3ft H and W

Long-season Flowers

Many flowering plants remain in bloom for only a short period, varying from a few days to several weeks. This is acceptable when they are chosen primarily for their foliage or are planted in a garden which is spacious enough to contain many different varieties ensuring successional blossom throughout the seasons. It is less welcome on a terrace or in a very small garden where space is at a premium. In this situation, one needs flowers which remain in beauty for a long while or are produced continuously over an extended period.

Campanula portenschlagiana (syn. *muralis*) E
Trailing bellflower with purplish blue flowers all summer. 10 × 45cm/4in × 1½ft. Some of the dwarf hybrids have an equally prolonged display like the lavender 'Birch Hybrid' (see page 100) or 'Stella', a form of *C. poscharskyana*.

Dianthus 'Doris' (Pink) E: ○
With its salmon-pink flowers and silvery leaves this
hybrid blooms all summer. It is a cultivar of the *Dianthus
allwoodii* group, short-lived but in perpetual bloom.
30cm/1ft H and W

Diascia vigilis ○
Showy warm pink flowers in summer cover the upright
spikes of a valuable though not fully hardy perennial.
30–45 × 60cm/1–1½ × 2ft

Geranium sanguineum var. **striatum** ○
Pink flowers cover wide mounds of leaves from early
summer till winter. There is also a white form called
'Album'. The type is magenta. 30 × 45cm/1 × 1½ft

Polyanthus
Individual blooms may be spoilt by wind and rain early
in the year. Wine, scarlet, pink, bronze, orange, yellow,
white, blue and violet forms can be raised from seed.
10 × 15cm/8 × 6in

***Osteospermum ecklonis* (African daisy)** ○
All osteospermums give a long display. This variety has
dark-centred shining white flowers produced en masse
from early summer until autumn frosts. A wonderful
display but the plant is not fully hardy and needs good
drainage. 30 × 45cm/1 × 1½ft

***Primula auricula*
(Auricula)**
Flowers are carried in
spring to early summer
above soft-green leaves. A
wide range of colour and
some varieties are dusted
with a white farina.
15cm/6in H and W

***Primula* 'Guinevere'**
With its bronzed leaves and yellow-eyed lilac flowers this
is amongst the most distinct primrose cultivars. But
there is a huge range amongst the primroses, both vivid
and subtle, and including laced petals and contrasting
speckling. 15cm/6in H and W

Viola cornuta E
This viola will flower from spring until frosts, especially
the white form, 'Alba', or the blue form, 'Lilacina'.
Other long-flowering violas include 'Bowles' Black', the
darkest; 'Irish Molly', lime-green and red; 'Jackanapes',
a yellow and mahogany bloom. 12 × 15cm/5 × 6in

***Campanula persicifolia*
'Telham Beauty' (Peach-
leafed bellflower)** E: ○
Blue cups all summer on
an easy plant, though best
in light soil. There is a
white form, self-sowing,
like the blue type plant.
1m × 30cm/3 × 1ft

Anemone* × *hybrida (syn. *A. japonica*)
Graceful and indispensable flowers which bloom from
late summer to autumn. There are both double and
single forms, white or pink. 75 × 45cm/2¹⁄₂ × 1¹⁄₂ft. The
form 'September Charm' is shorter at 45cm/1¹⁄₂ft.

Coreopsis verticillata ○
A reliable and clump-forming spreader with delicate
foliage and an unending succession of dazzling golden
daisy flowers throughout the summer. 60 × 45cm/
2 × 1¹⁄₂ft

***Fuchsia* 'Lena'**
Fairly hardy pink and
purple cultivar in
continuous bloom from
summer until frosts.
60 × 45cm/2 × 1¹⁄₂ft. In
mild districts the plants
will grow large as they are
shrubs; in cold districts,
they will be cut to the
ground each winter and
live the life of herbaceous
plants.

LONG-SEASON
FLOWERS:
PERENNIALS UP TO
1M/3FT

CONSIDER ALSO:

Aster × frikartii p.161
Centaurea hypoleuca
 'John Coutts' p.161
Dahlia p.170
Dianthus deltoides p.96
Salvia × superba p.165
Many annual and half-
hardy annuals are also
suitable, including
Begonia semperflorens,
Cleome, *Cosmos*,
Nasturtium, *Impatiens*
(busy lizzie), *Nicotiana*
and *Verbena*.
See also the long-
season annuals shown
on pages 154–5.

Penstemon ○
Sub-shrubs for well-drained, fertile soil. Not all are
hardy but 'Garnet', a dark red, is fairly reliable. White,
red and purple cultivars are obtainable. 'Cherry Ripe'
and the scarlet 'Firebird' are forms of *P. hartwegii* which
flower from summer till autumn. 60 × 45cm/2 × 1½ft

***Tradescantia virginiana*
'Purple Dome'
(Spiderwort)**
Three-petalled flowers all
summer till frosts.
Varieties include white
with a blue centre in the
form 'Osprey', violet-blue
in 'Isis', mauve-blue in
'J.C. Weguelin'. 45cm/1½ft
H and W

***Linum narbonense* 'Heavenly Blue'** ○
Intense sky-blue flowers all summer on wiry stems.
Group for a brilliant display. Best on rich, light soils,
but even in these conditions the plant tends to be
short-lived. 45 × 30cm/1½ × 1ft

Hydrangea in variety ◗
Examples include *H. serrata* 'Grayswood'
(above left), a neat shrub to 1.2m/4ft H
and W, its blue and white lace-caps
changing from white to pink in summer
and finally deep crimson in autumn; or

'Preziosa' with domed pink heads ageing
to claret: 1.5m/5ft H and W. Of the mop-
heads, *H. macrophylla* 'Hamburg' (above
right) with rosy florets has a long season.
1.8×2.4m/6×8ft

Lavatera '**Barnsley**' ○
Fast growing with palest pink flowers all summer and
downy leaves. Not fully hardy and best in well-drained,
poorish soil to stop any tendency to run to leaf.
1.8m/6ft H and W

***Potentilla fruticosa*
'Elizabeth'**
Primrose flowers over a
dense mound from late
spring until frosts. 1m/3ft
H and W. 'Tangerine' is
rich orange; 'Red Ace' is
the closest to red.
'Abbotswood' is white.

Romneya coulteri ○
Large white flowers with golden stamens from summer onwards, and grey-green leaves. It can be difficult to establish, but where happy, it can invade a border.
1.5/5ft × indefinite spread

English roses combine the repeat-flowering habit of modern-bush roses with the sumptuous, many-petalled flowers of the old roses. 'Sweet Juliet' (above) is a very fragrant example with a strong upright leafy habit. 1.2 × 1m/4 × 3ft

Roses: Floribunda ○
The Floribunda group contains some of the most floriferous and perpetual roses such as 'Escapade' (above) with fragrant, white-centred rosy-lilac flowers. Vigorous, bushy and healthy. 1.2m/4ft H and W. Consider also 'Amber Queen', a beautiful Floribunda, shown on p. 123.

Floribundas were preceded by Polyantha Pompons, smaller but with continuity of bloom also; of these 'Natalie Nypels' (above) has semi-double, fragrant pink flowers till winter. 1m/3ft H and W

Clematis 'Jackmanii Superba'
Velvety purple flowers, larger than those on the usual ×
jackmanii plant are produced prolifically from summer
to early autumn. Up to 6m/20ft. See also clematis on pp.
222–3.

Eccremocarpus scaber ○
Fast-growing plant but not reliably hardy. Little
orange-red (or yellow) tubular flowers all summer till
frost. Bi-pinnate leaves on stems to 4.5m. Easy from
seed.

Jasminum officinale ○
Small, fragrant white flowers in clusters all summer.
Green or variegated leaves on a popular old climber
that prefers sun but tolerates almost any soil. Vigorous
to 7m/23ft

Rosa 'Golden Showers'
This rose tolerates part-shaded walls and has a long
season, bearing bright yellow semi-double flowers fading
to cream. 3m/10ft
Consider also *R.* 'Mermaid' on p. 224.

Other long-flowering
shrubs and climbers
include:

Cobaea scandens p.150
Fremontodendron
  'California Glory'
  p.222
Hydrangea arborescens
  'Grandiflora' p.201
Ipomoea p.150
Thunbergia alata p.150

Rosa 'Climbing Iceberg' ○
Few climbing roses can be termed fully perpetual, but
this climbing form of the floribunda, provides
recurrent flushes of its white flowers over glossy pale
green leaves from early summer to autumn. 4m/13ft

Temporary Effects: Annuals, Pots etc.

In any confined space, one needs a change of plants to avoid the monotony of looking at the same scene day after day. Annuals and half-hardy annuals are temporary residents and will give an abundance of flower and/or lushness of foliage that only the warm weather makes possible.

The most useful are those annuals with a long season in flower and also those plants which perform well in pots and tubs. Plant annuals in bare pockets or areas, or sow the longer-flowering varieties in the empty spaces of any missing paving stones, so long as the soil is friable. Consider also using tender, rapid-growing climbers either to fill spaces on walls or to festoon large shrubs or to conceal structural eyesores etc. before permanent plants have begun to cover them.

Most annuals will flourish only in full sun, but a few in the lists on these pages will thrive in shadier positions.

Cobaea scandens ○
Tender perennial grown as a half-hardy annual. Purple bells or cream in the form 'Alba'. Gives dense coverage, but needs support. May sprint to 6m/20ft in the season.

Ipomoea rubro caerulea ○
This is the blue morning glory. Other forms have deep violet, carmine or white flowers, or striped or variegated blooms or leaves. Grown as a half-hardy annual, but blooms well only in warm summers. Support is necessary. 3m/10ft

Lathyrus odoratus (**Sweet pea**) ○
There is a large colour range of this hardy annual, including bi-colours. All are fragrant. The antique varieties are even more scented but tend to have small flowers and an untidy habit of growth. 1.8m/6ft

Nasturtium (*Tropaeolum*) ○
The climbing form flowers all summer in a range of yellows and reds. Will trail to give ground-cover or climb on a trellis, shrubs or a hedge. One of its virtues is that it will do well on poor, dry soil. Hardy annual. 1.8m/6ft

Thunbergia alata ○
Thin climber with cream or orange flowers with a black centre, or white with a yellow centre in the form 'Angel Wings'. Blooms for a long period. Support with a wire trellis or canes, or use as a trailing plant in a container. Tender perennial grown as a half-hardy annual. May reach 2.4m/8ft.

Abutilon hybrids ◑
Shrubby plants which can be flowered as half-hardy annuals. Beautifully veined, open bell-flowers in cream, yellow, primrose, pink, scarlet or wine shades. Tender. 1m × 60cm/3 × 2ft

Agave americana E: ◑
Frost-tender succulent with a blue-grey rosette of leaves with fierce spines. *A.a.* 'Marginata' is shown here, a striking gold-variegated form. 45cm/1½ft H and W. Position the potted plants with caution to avoid injury, and better omit them altogether where there are children or pets.

Amaranthus caudatus (Love-lies-bleeding)
A distinctive hardy annual with trailing maroon (or green in the form 'Viridis') long flower tassels from late summer to autumn. Can self-sow. 60 × 45cm/ 2 × 1½ft

Datura (syn. *Brugmansia*) *fastuosa* (syn. *metel*) ◑
Large single or double, scented trumpets of white, violet or pale yellow on a tender, bushy plant to 1m × 60cm/3 × 2ft. Can be flowered as half-hardy annual. The white and fragrant *D. suaveolens* shown here is impressive grown as a standard for a big tub. All are poisonous. 1.8 × 1m/6 × 3ft

***Heliotropium peruvianum*
(Cherry pie)** ○
This tender perennial is
very strongly perfumed. It
looks well in a pot
positioned against silver
foliage. 45cm/1½ft
H and W

***Eucomis bicolor* (Pineapple plant)**
A spectacular bulb with long-lasting though initially
unpleasantly smelling flowers in midsummer and
attractive green seed-capsules. Not fully hardy.
45cm/1½ft

***Fuchsia* 'Thalia'**
A graceful tender fuchsia
with tubular, red flowers.
Very floriferous from
summer through till
autumn. 60cm/2ft H and
W. Good tender hybrids
include 'Dollar Princess'
(rich purple corolla and
crimson sepals), and
'Coachman' (deep salmon
corolla, pink sepals).

***Pelargonium* 'Madame Layal' (Geranium)** ○
A very pretty cultivar that belongs to the Angel group
with distinctively zoned flowers like small pansies. A
good small tender perennial for a pot. 30cm/1ft
H and W

***Ricinus communis* (Castor-oil plant)** ○
A tender perennial that is grown as a half-hardy annual.
The form usually grown is 'Gibsonii' or 'Impala' with
large bronzed leaves and small orange flower clusters.
Poisonous seeds. 1.5 × 1m/5 × 3ft

Asarina **'Victoria Falls'** ○
A tender tuberous perennial with soft green leaves and brilliant magenta trumpets which will cascade along its stems for most of the summer. Trailing to 45cm/1½ft

Helichrysum petiolare ○
A tender grey-leafed perennial which is indispensable for a hanging basket. Its cool coloured foliage is a foil to brighter companions. To 45cm/1½ft

Fuchsia **'Pink Galore'**
A cascading shy-branching double fuchsia which is not too vigorous for a basket and will flower from summer to autumn. Trailing to 45cm/1½ft

Lotus berthelotii ○
A spectacular silver filigree-leafed plant with scarlet claw flowers is an unusual and dramatic addition to a hanging basket. To 60cm/2ft

Pelargonium **'Roller's Pioneer' (Ivy-leafed geranium)** ○
These tender perennials will tolerate drought as they are slightly succulent. This form has marbled-leaves, a marking that is called crocodile. Trailing to 60cm/2ft

Verbena ○
There are several named varieties of which 'Sissinghurst' is one of the most popular with an unending succession of bright pink flowers from summer to autumn at the end of its trailing stems. To 40cm/1ft 4in

Begonia semperflorens
A fibrous-rooted begonia
grown as a half-hardy
annual, though a tender
perennial. Colours include
white, pink, scarlet or bi-
colours and bronze or
green foliage. Blooms all
summer until frosts and
will also tolerate shade.
15 × 20cm/6 × 8in

Anagallis monellii ○
Gentian blue flowers with a
red eye twinkle on a dwarf
bushy tender perennial,
usually grown as a half-
hardy annual which flowers
unendingly from summer
until autumn. 15cm/6in
H and W

Antirrhinum (**Snapdragon**) ○
Short-lived perennial best grown as a half-hardy annual.
Single or double flowers in shades of yellow, orange,
pink, scarlet, wine and white. 15cm–1m × 30cm/
6in–3ft × 1ft

Arctotis **hybrids (African daisy)** ○
Bushy plants with daisy-flowers in shades
of cream, yellow, pink or crimson.
45cm/1½ft H and W. Grown as half-hardy
annuals.

Cosmos ○
Graceful ferny-leafed plants with large
single flowers of crimson, rose or white
over a long season. Also gold or orange
variety with two rows of petals growing to
75 × 30cm/2½ × 1ft.

Impatiens hybrids (**Busy Lizzie**)
A valuable tender perennial for moist sun or shade, blooming continuously all summer. Usually single flowers in red, white, mauve, orange or pink, though there is also a rose-like, double-flowered form in the same colour range. This will not tolerate full shade. 30cm–1m/1–3ft H and W

Osteospermum hybrids
(**African daisy**) ○
Satiny blooms in apricot, cream, lemon or white, pink and violet. Sow late as a hardy annual or grow as a half-hardy.
30 × 25cm/1ft × 10in

Nemesia fruticans
This little perennial, though not fully hardy, will self-seed and return next year. 10 × 15cm/ 8 × 6in

Nicotiana (**Tobacco flower**)
Indispensable, perfumed flowers of white, lime-green, crimson or dusky pink though some forms will not open their blossoms fully in daylight. Good in part-shade. The taller varieties have more grace.
45cm–1m × 45cm/1½–3ft × 1½ft

Petunia ○
Single or double flowers in an extensive colour range, including many lurid bi-colors. Grown as a half-hardy annual, will bloom all summer till frosts. Must have full sun and are very resistant to drought. 22 × 15cm/9 × 6in

Verbena ○
Edging plants which have a long flowering season, and are weather-resistant. Purple, lavender, red, pink or white flowers; *V. venosa* has rosy-purple flowers and produces tubers which can be lifted and stored. 45 × 30cm/1½ × 1ft

The plants on these pages are virtually foolproof to grow from seed. Moreover their variety makes them highly adaptable, some suited to fill a summer border in a new garden, others to occupy gaps after a death or before permanent plants have grown to their allotted span. Some will also act as charming edging plants.

Echium (E. vulgare) ○
Blue (also rose, mauve or white), long-flowering, easy, and bushy plants for edges or the rock garden. The form shown is called 'Blue Bedder'. 30cm/1ft H and W

Eschscholzia ○
The California poppy has showy single or double flowers of red, mauve, pink, orange, yellow and cream with a long season. Good for poor, dry soils. 15–30 × 15cm/6in–1ft × 6in

Godetia
There are many varieties with single or double flowers in white, salmon, lilac, pink or carmine. Hardy annuals which are best in full sun but do quite well in part-shade. 30–60cm × 15–30cm/1–2ft × 6in–1ft

Nigella damascena (**Love-in-a-mist**) ○
Beautiful, easy annual with feathery foliage and white, rose, dark blue or pale blue flowers (this is the finest cultivar, called 'Miss Jekyll'), followed by handsome seed pods. 37 × 15cm/1ft 3in × 6in

Planting a Border

Planting a border or a bed is one of the great pleasures. You are creating a picture out of a collection of plants and the possibilities are infinite. Lacy foliage against bold leaves, harmonies or contrasts of colour will make their own collective impact. Organized variety is what you seek. And if you choose carefully, a border can be stunning as well as easy to tend.

Labour-saving Perennials

One criticism levelled at the mixed border is that it involves its owner in hard work to make it prosper. This need not be true. A mixed border is easy to maintain so long as its inmates are carefully selected with this aim in mind. Plan it along the lines suggested on page 8, and when you come to choose hardy perennials, pick them from the following list. All the plants in this section have been chosen not only for their beauty but also for their labour-saving qualities. You won't need to stake them or lift and divide them regularly to keep them flourishing. If you give them the conditions they need, and mulch as required, they will thrive undisturbed in the same position for many years, and there are some which insist on being left alone for ever.

Agapanthus **'Headbourne Hybrids'** ○
Handsome, relatively hardy clump-forming plants bearing large heads of deep or pale blue tubular flowers in mid-late summer. 75cm/2¹⁄₂ft H and W

Aruncus dioicus **'Kneiffii'** ◑
Mound-forming, cut-leafed foliage plant with creamy plumes of starry flowers in mid-summer. Part-shade and good, moist soil. 1m × 60cm/3 × 2ft

Aquilegia **'Snow Queen'**
White spurred flowers for early summer (for several months if dead-headed). Big colour range among other border hybrids. Short-lived perennials, best in light soil and longest flowering in part-shade. 60 × 45cm/2 × 1¹⁄₂ft

Astilbe ◗

Needs good, moist soil and part shade. There are many hybrids flowering in summer with a colour range through ruby, scarlet, pink and white. 'Erica', illustrated here, is 1m/3ft H and W.

Astrantia major

Easy, clump-forming plant in sun or shade with pin-cushion flowers surrounded by bracts. 60 × 45cm/ 2 × 1½ft. *A. maxima* is slightly more compact and has pinkish flowers with rosy bracts. Both flower for a long period in summer.

Aster × frikartii ○

The easiest and one of the prettiest asters with lavender-blue flowers from midsummer until autumn. 75 × 45cm/2½ × 1½ft

Centaurea hypoleuca 'John Coutts' ○

Pink cornflowers throughout the summer above greyish leaves. Spreading plant which needs good drainage. 60 × 45cm/2 × 1½ft

Geranium 'Johnson's Blue'
A most accommodating
clump-forming perennial
with intense violet-blue
flowers in summer over a
mound of ground-
covering foliage.
30 × 60cm/1 × 2ft

Geranium psilostemon (syn. *armenum*) ○
This bushy geranium has dark-eyed and very showy
magenta flowers in summer. Leaves colour hotly in
autumn. A light self-seeder in sun. Up to 1m/3ft H and
W. See also the geraniums on pages 105, 173 and 174.

***Dicentra spectabilis* (Bleeding heart)** ◑
Beautiful, spring-border plant with heart-shaped
rose-pink flowers. Most reliable in moist but well-
drained soil and part-shade. There is a lovely white
variety called 'Alba' which requires the same
conditions. 60 × 45cm/2 × 1½ft

***Euphorbia griffithii* 'Fireglow'** ○
This spurge is a fine cultivar with brick-red flower heads
in early summer and strong, bushy spreading growth.
75 × 45cm/2½ × 1½ft. Other easy border candidates
include *E. polychroma* (p. 60) and *E. characias ssp. wulfenii*
(p. 55).

Hemerocallis **'Pink Damask' (Day lily)**
A reliable border plant producing a prolonged
succession of summer flowers and handsome rushy
leaves. Adaptable and easy. Innumerable cream, yellow,
mahogany-red and pink cultivars exist ranging
60cm–1m × 60cm/2–3ft × 2ft.

Iris sibirica ○
Arguably the easiest and
best iris species for the
border. Cultivars of white,
blue, plum or violet
obtainable. Moist soil
preferred. The
photograph shows 'Snow
Bounty'. All flower in high
summer. 1m × 60cm/
3 × 2ft

Lilium regale
The easy and fragrant regal lily which is lime-tolerant.
It needs planting deeply as it is stem-rooting. Summer-
flowering. The form 'Album' differs only in that it is
fully white rather than having a purple-flush on the
outside of the flowers. Up to 1.2m × 30cm/4 × 1ft

Mertensia virginica ◐
A beautiful, spring-
flowering, spreading plant
for a cool soil and part-
shade. Greyish leaves die
down early. 45cm/1½ft
H and W

Lychnis chalcedonica **(Maltese cross)** ○
A true scarlet-flowered plant which needs light soil to
thrive. It flowers in high summer. There are few other
border plants of this colour. 1m × 45cm/3 × 1½ft

Peonies ○
Essential border plants. Although their burst of flowers
in early summer is short-lived, their foliage persists
attractively. Of the different groups and many cultivars,
the photograph shows *Paeonia lactiflora* 'Bowl of
Beauty' 1m/3ft H and W. Never disturb peonies.

Polemonium reptans **'Lambrook Mauve'** ○
A low-growing form of Jacob's ladder with attractive
deep green foliage and clusters of lilac flowers en masse
in early summer. 60cm/2ft H and W

Rudbeckia fulgida 'Goldsturm' ○
A vigorous cultivar, dwarfer than most which flowers from summer till autumn, producing a prolific display of golden, black-centred daisies. 75 × 45cm/2½ × 1½ft

Salvia × superba ○
A robust, long-flowering plant with violet-purple spikes in summer.
1m × 45cm/3 × 1½ft. 'East Friesland' is a shorter cultivar at 45 cm/1½ft. 'May Night', illustrated here also 45cm/1½ft, begins to flower slightly earlier.

Sisyrinchium striatum E: ○
Iris-like leaves and pale yellow spires of flowers in early summer. Good contrast to a horizontal-leafed neighbour.
60 × 22.5cm/2ft × 9in

Sedum 'Autumn Joy' ○
A most reliable, robust plant with succulent leaves and flat heads of russet flowers in autumn.
45cm/1½ft H and W

Sidalcea ○
Spikes of mallow-like flowers of pink or red over a long season in summer. Leave undisturbed as long as possible. 75cm–1m × 45cm/2½–3ft × 1½ft depending on cultivar.

CONSIDER ALSO:

Anemone × hybrida
  p.144
Artemisia 'Lambrook
  Silver' p.68
Bergenia p.52
Brunnera macrophylla
  p.92
Epimedium p.104
Helleborus orientalis
  p.137
Hosta p.61
Kniphofia p.55
Nepeta × faassenii p.69
Tradescantia p.145

BORDER PERENNIALS

The plants on these pages demand a little more attention than those on the previous list.

Anchusa azurea 'Loddon Royalist' ○
One of the most intensely blue border perennials with sprays of small flowers in early summer and coarse hairy leaves. Stake 1.2m × 60cm/4 × 2ft

***Alstroemeria* 'Ligtu hybrids'** ○
Gorgeous summer flower–carmine to cream to salmon. Spreading where happy but can be hard to establish. Plant container-grown subjects and never disturb. Give rich soil and twiggy support to the taller cultivars. 30cm–1m × 60cm/1–3 × 2ft

Campanula lactiflora
White, pink and lavender cultivars obtainable, and a rich blue called 'Prichard's Variety', which flower in summer, often until autumn. For moist, rich soil. Stake tall plants and do not disturb. 1.4m × 75cm/4 × 2½ft

Dendranthema (syn. *Chrysanthemum*) **'Ruby Mound'** ○
A mass of glowing red flowers light the garden in autumn. 1.2m × 45cm/4 × 1½ft. Most chrysanthemums benefit from regular division and twiggy support.

Dierama pulcherrimum **(Angel's fishing-rod; Wandflower)** ○
This graceful plant prefers light neutral to acid soil. Pink, rose or maroon bells in late summer over rushy leaves. Not fully hardy. 1m × 45cm/3 × 1½ft

Delphinium ○
There are many named cultivars or, grown from seed, the Pacific Giant series in pink, white or pale to darkest blue, but these may dwindle after a few years.
1.2–1.8m × 60cm–1m/4–6ft × 2–3ft. 'Belladonna' varieties are shorter. Rich, moist soil and staking needed.

Eremurus bungei ○
One of the magnificent fox-tail lilies, whose crowns and shoots are frost-tender and need protection before they emerge in spring. Avoid disturbance after planting as the roots are brittle. 1.5m × 45cm/ 5 × 1½ft

Helenium ○
The most useful cultivars are those that flower from
late summer through the autumn, such as the crimson-
bronze 'Bruno' or the bronze-red 'Moorheim Beauty'
illustrated here. Stake these taller varieties if they are
in windy positions. 1m × 45cm/2 × 1½ft

Kirengeshoma palmata ◐ ●

A beautiful pale yellow, autumn-flowering, Japanese plant for shade and moist, leafy soil where it can spread. Good companion to shade-loving shrubs. 75 × 60cm/2½ × 2ft

Meconopsis betonicifolia LH: ◐
The Himalayan poppy has sky-blue poppy flowers in summer and hairy, glaucous leaves. Only perennial if plants are stopped from flowering in their first year: 1m × 4cm/3 × 1½ft. *M. × sheldonii* is a deeper blue. All need cool, leafy soil and part shade.

Lupinus hybrid (**Lupin**) ○
Peppery-scented pea-flowers in summer. It is sometimes prone to mildew. 1m × 60cm/3 × 2ft

***Monarda* 'Croftway Pink'** ○
A pretty cultivar of bergamot, a showy plant with flowers of red, pink, violet or white in summer to autumn. Regular division is beneficial. For moist but well-drained soil. 1m × 60cm/3 × 2ft

***Papaver orientale*
'Charming'** ○
A pale-flowered form of the oriental poppy, all of which have showy flowers of pink, red, orange or white in early summer, often with a black base to the petals. Stake and cut down the untidy foliage after flowering. Don't disturb. 1m × 75cm/3 × 2ft

***Phlox paniculata* 'Little Lovely'** ◐
A shorter-growing example of the scented phlox, which has late summer flowers of lavender, purple, pink, red, salmon, or white. Needs moist soil and prefers part-shade. Division every three years necessary. Often menaced by eelworm. 60cm–1m × 60cm/ 2–3ft × 2ft

In cold regions, all the following plants will need lifting or protection during the winter.

Dahlia merckii ○
A graceful variety that is very different from the showy fat-flowered cultivars grown in most borders. It blooms from summer until autumn. The tubers may need lifting for the winter, or give them a thick winter-covering in a sheltered place if left in the ground. 1m/3ft H and W

Lobelia **'Dark Crusader'** ○
Rich red velvety flowers in late summer distinguish this tender perennial, which enjoys moist soil. In cold regions the crowns will need covering for winter protection. 1m × 30cm/3 × 1ft

Felicia amelloides ○
The brilliant blue yellow-eyed kingfisher daisy will make
a sparkling small bush all summer to autumn, if it can
be lifted and brought through the winter. 45cm/1½ft
H and W

Salvia buchananii ○
One of the sages with magenta lipped, velvety flowers in
summer and glossy dark green leaves. It will need
protection under glass in winter. If it is dead-headed, it
will produce flowers over a longer period.
60cm/2ft H and W

Salvia patens ○
Rich azure flowers are produced throughout the
summer on this tuberous perennial which has softly
hairy leaves. Lift the tubers before winter or give
them frost protection in the ground. 60cm/2ft
H and W

Edge-breakers

No bed or border ever looks luxuriant or even comfortable if it stops short of its edge. The plants seem self-conscious, as though they are only perching there but have not taken root and settled in. This stiff appearance can be avoided if you plant along the edge the kind of spreading subjects which will spill over the boundary. The most useful plants are evergreen, but there are also many herbaceous candidates with lush, bold leaves and arching stems which will be effective from spring to autumn. For the shrub border, the most valuable are either the less rampant prostrate evergreen shrubs or else those under 1m/3ft with a rounded habit which will sit like hummocks at and over the edge. To simplify mowing the adjacent lawn lay a line of paving (mowing-stones) at the edge of the bed below the level of the grass.

Artemisia canescens Semi-E: ○
A splendid bushy perennial with very finely cut leaves curling like silver wire. It will make good ground cover. 45cm/1½ft H and W

Campanula alliariifolia
Clump-forming perennial with long, heart-shaped, grey-green leaves and stems of ivory flowers for many weeks in summer and intermittently in autumn. 45cm/1½ft H and W

***Dianthus* 'Mrs Sinkins'** ○
One of the favourite old pinks, with a messily-presented flower as it often bursts its calyx, yet so heavily scented that it is still grown. 15 × 25cm/6 × 10in

EDGE-BREAKERS: PERENNIALS FOR SUN

Geranium cinereum 'Ballerina' ○
Appealing rosetted perennial with dusky pink, dark-eyed and dark-veined flowers in early summer onwards for a long period. 10 × 30cm/4in × 1ft

CONSIDER ALSO:

Anthemis cupaniana p.214
Carex comans p.86
Geranium p.105
Helictotrichon sempervirens p.86
Hemerocallis p.82
Nepeta × faassenii p.69
Stachys byzantina p.69
Stipa gigantea p.87

Hakonechloa macra 'Alboaurea' ○
A golden Japanese grass with some green and fawn variegation. Yellowish inflorescence in late summer. A dazzling low edger. 45cm/1½ft H and W

Liriope muscari E: ○
Valuable, labour-saving plant with rushy evergreen leaves and spikes of small violet flowers over a long period late in the year. 30cm/1ft H and W

Veronica austriaca ssp. **teucrium 'Corfu Form'**
A good edge-breaker for a low wall or a bank where its sprays of intensely blue small flowers will mass the plant in early summer. 20 × 30cm/10 × 1ft

173

Ferns E: ◑
The evergreen *Polystichum setiferum* 'Divisilobum' is illustrated here with its lacy, finely divided fronds, one of the best of the ground spraying ferns. Needs well-drained soil. 50 × 60cm/1ft 8in × 2ft. The deciduous *Athyrium* (p. 53) and evergreen hart's tongue fern (p. 110) are also first choices.

Geranium clarkei **'Kashmir White'**
A graceful perennial with white mauve-veined drooping flowers in summer held over a mound of finely cut leaves which make spreading ground-cover. 30 × 45cm/1 × 1½ft

Geranium macrorrhizum **'Bevan's Variety'**
A groundcover plant with aromatic leaves that colour richly in autumn and magenta flowers in spring to early summer. Other forms have white or lilac flowers. It will self-seed. 30cm/1ft H and W

Hosta 'Frances Williams' ◐
A very handsome cultivar making a mound of ribbed leaves which are greyish-green with yellow edges, fading with age. It has lilac flowers in summer. 75cm/2½ft H and W

CONSIDER ALSO:

Alchemilla mollis p.52
Bergenia p.52
Campanula 'Birch
 Hybrid' p.100
Helleborus foetidus
 p.113
H. orientalis p.137
Hosta in variety
Tellima grandiflora
 p.105

EDGE-BREAKERS: SHADE-TOLERANT PERENNIALS

Saxifraga × *urbium* (**London pride**) E: ○ ◐ ●
This neat accommodating plant is happy wherever it is grown. Its prostrate leaf rosettes will spread to form a neat edging over paving. It has pale or deep pink sprays of starry flowers in late spring/early summer. There is also a variegated form. 25cm/10in × indefinite spread

Heuchera (Alum root) E: ◐
Virtually evergreen leaves surmounted by dainty flowers of white, cream, pink or shades of red in early summer. The photograph shows *H*. 'Rachel'.
45 × 30cm/1½ × 1ft

***Philadelphus* 'Manteau d'Hermine'**
A compact domed mock orange, covered with scented white double flowers in early to midsummer. It will make a pouffe at the front of a shrub or mixed border. 1 × 1.5m/3 × 5ft

Ballota pseudodictamnus E: ○
A sub-shrub with soft and hairy grey-green rounded leaves and whorls of tiny pink flowers and green calyces. It is not fully hardy and needs a well-drained soil. 60cm × 1m/ 2 × 3ft

> CONSIDER ALSO:
>
> *Artemisia* 'Powis Castle' p.88
> *Helianthemum* p.96
> Lavender p.207
> *Ruta graveolens* p.71

***Hebe* 'Pewter Dome'** E: ○
There are a number of valuable evergreen hebes for this position. This one makes a spreading, grey, small-leafed mound with white flower-spikes in summer. 75cm × 1m/2½ × 3ft. See also *H. rakaiensis* (syn. *subalpina*) on page 107.

***Picea pungens glauca* 'Procumbens'** E
Stunningly blue, prostrate spruce which is suited to the front of a conifer- or rock-border. Its stiffness makes it an alien in the conventional setting of the mixed, deciduous border. 15cm × 1m/6in × 3ft

Penstemon glaber Semi-E: ○
A wonderful sub-shrub for ground-cover, with blue and pink flowerbells for a long period in summer. It is reasonably hardy in a sheltered position, but the old flowering stems should not be cut back until spring. 40 × 60cm/1ft 4in × 2ft

Salvia lavandulifolia E: ○
A bushy sage with slender greyish-green leaves and sprays of mauve flowers that make a great show in summer. It needs well-drained soil as it is not fully hardy. 75cm/2½ft H and W

***Santolina rosmarinifolia ssp. rosmarinifolia* (Green cotton lavender)** E: ○
Rich green leaves and flat flower-heads in summer. Will spread out, but a number grouped together will form a fuller mound. 45cm/1½ft H and W

Daphne pontica E ◑ ●
This shrub makes an increasingly spreading dome of
neat evergreen foliage with very scented lime-yellow
flowers in spring. 1 × 1.2m/3 × 4ft

Consider also the
smaller, bushy
hydrangeas such as *H.*
'Preziosa'; also *Skimmia*
japonica p.127 and
Viburnum davidii p.109.

Rhododendron: Azalea E: LH: ◑
The most suitable azaleas for edging positions are the
spring-flowering, evergreen varieties which form
spreading bushes of 60cm–1.2m/2–4ft. There is a
colour range of white, pink, red, orange, lavender and
violet. 'Hinomayo' shown here, is a Japanese hybrid,
belonging to the Kurume group, an old and reliable
variety massed with clear pink flowers in late spring.
60cm × 1m/2 × 3ft

Rhododendron E: LH: ◑
Of the thousands of this genus under cultivation, the
most useful in a front-of-border position are those
which have a neat, mounded habit. Of these, *R.*
williamsianum (above) is an exquisite species with heart-
shaped leaves and pale pink or white bell flowers in
spring. 60cm × 1.2m/2 × 4ft

Back-of-border Shrubs

The back of a border is a position best reserved for certain kinds of plants. First, for the tallest, most corpulent shrubs which will act as a visual stop and a background to the plants in front. Second, for frost-tender or doubtfully hardy plants which will be safer if protected by a wall or fence. Third, for shrubs which bloom at a cold season of the year and whose blossoms will be less vulnerable here to bad weather. Fourth, for the kind of tall or medium-size old favourites like lilacs or buddlejas, with beautiful flowers but undistinguished foliage or habit. Fifth, for climbers or semi-scandent shrubs which need either the support of a wall or a large plant to entwine. Lastly, a high proportion of evergreens is essential here, especially if the border is much in view from the house during winter; for this group of plants, see especially pages 48–51 and the large evergreens on pages 62–7.

Abutilon × suntense ○
A beautiful hybrid abutilon which is only frost hardy. It bears in profusion rich mauve saucer-flowers in early summer and has grey-green foliage.
3m × 1.8m/10 × 6ft

Abutilon vitifolium ○
Equally beautiful with greyish foliage and either soft lavender (or white in the form 'Album') flowers in early summer. Not fully hardy. 3 × 1.8m/10 × 6ft

Buddleja crispa ○
A soft felted grey foliaged shrub with lilac orange-throated flowers for a long period in summer to autumn. Not fully hardy. 2.4m/8ft H and W

Callistemon rigidus E: ○
An Australian shrub with rich red-stamened bottlebrush flowers in early summer. In cold-winter areas it needs to be trained on a wall for greater shelter where it may reach 3m/10ft.

Clianthus puniceus
(Lobster claw plant) Semi-
E: ○
Gorgeous tender wall-
shrub with ferny foliage
and coral (or white)
pendent flowers in
summer. Best trained on a
wire-mesh support. Up to
3m/10ft

CONSIDER ALSO:

Carpenteria californica
  p.50
Ceanothus in variety
  p.50
Cistus in variety p.122
Choisya ternata p.48
Cytisus battandieri p.72
Fremontodendron
  'Californian Glory'
  p.222
Solanum crispum
  'Glasnevin' p.229

Ceanothus **'Trewithen Blue'** E or semi-E: ○
One of the more tender ceanothus with large panicles of
rich blue flowers in early summer. Vigorous to 6m/20ft
H and W

Escallonia **'Iveyi'** E: ○
A vigorous, bushy
evergreen with shining
leaves and showy panicles
of small white flowers from
summer to autumn. Not
fully hardy. 4 × 3m/
13 × 10ft

Hoheria lyallii ○
A large grey-green leafed shrub or small tree which will
need pruning on wall space. An avalanche of fragrant
small white flowers in summer. 4 × 3m/13 × 10ft

Itea ilicifolia E: ○
An evergreen shrub with
holly-like leaves and long
ice-green fragrant catkin
inflorescences in summer
to 30cm/1ft or more. Not
fully hardy. 3m/10ft H and
W

Buddleja davidii **(Butterfly bush)** ○
A shrub with a leggy habit and long scented panicles in
summer of lavender, white, purple-red or dark purple.
The form shown is 'Dartmoor' presenting its flowers in
multiple plumes. 3 × 2.1m/10 × 7ft

Cotoneaster horizontalis
This will lean its way up a
wall where it is notable for
its attractive fish-bone
habit. Insignificant white
flowers in spring followed
by showy red berries in
autumn. A form with
cream-variegated leaves is
obtainable. Up to 4m/13ft
on a wall.

***Chaenomeles* × *superba* 'Pink Lady'** **(Japonica)**
A spring-blooming shrub which does well if it is trained
as a wall-specimen. It should be pruned after flowering,
reducing side shoots to 2 or 3 buds. To 1.8m/6ft on a
wall.

Syringa 'Missumo' (Lilac) ○
There are many cultivars
of this familiar large shrub,
with single or double
scented flowers of pink,
lilac-blue, purple, white or
lemon in early summer.
5m/16ft H and W

Paeonia delavayi var. ludlowii ○
The largest tree peony with elegantly cut foliage and
glowing golden bowls of flowers in early summer. Shield
shoots in early spring from morning sun and frost.
2.4m/8ft H and W

Philadelphus 'Belle Etoile' (Mock orange) ○
One of the loveliest scented philadelphus with a dark
staining at the base of its petals. It flowers in summer.
2.1m/7ft H and W

Syringa × josiflexa 'Bellicent' ○
A Canadian hybrid lilac with large plumes of graceful
pendent pink flowers in early summer. It is very
fragrant. 4 × 5m/13 × 16ft

Perennials for Pool Borders or Moist Sites

There are many plants which actually need conditions that are permanently moist in order to thrive. These are a gardener's first choice when it comes to planting a bog garden or the margins of a pool or a stream. They are a varied and handsome lot. Some of these plants have bold architectural leaves and are equally attractive whether in or out of flower. Others, such as those from the primula family, include some of the most beautiful flowers one can grow. If you are making a pool border, it is a good idea to choose a proportion which spray over the edges of the pool and form green waterfalls themselves. This ensures they will conceal the ugly join between water and earth (or liner).

***Caltha palustris* 'Flore Pleno'** ○
A double form of the marsh marigold which forms bold clumps of gold in spring above dark green leaves. It is not quite as spreading as the single form. 30cm/1ft H and W

***Darmera peltata* (Umbrella plant)**
Handsome, spreading foliage plant for moist soil round larger pools. Pink sprays of flowers in spring followed by large round leaves, usually colouring well in autumn. Good companion for grassy-leafed plants. 1m × 60cm/ 3 × 2ft

Gunnera manicata
Giant-leafed waterside subject for large areas. Its inflorescences appear in early summer. Establish in spring and cover crowns in winter with its dead leaves as frost-protection. It is not fully hardy. 3m/10ft H and W

Iris ensata (syn. *kaempferi*)
LH
The Japanese iris has most beautiful velvety flowers in midsummer of purple, blue, mauve, red or white. It can be tricky as it needs plenty of water when growing but drier conditions in winter.
1m × 30cm/3 × 1ft

Iris pseudacorus
'Bastardii'
The variegated form of the wild yellow flag, which produces golden flowers in early summer. It is less invasive than the self-seeding plain green form which is only suited to larger areas.
1.2m × 30cm/4 × 1ft

***Iris versicolor* 'Kermesina'**
A lovely North American with plum-purple flowers
veined and marked with gold in early summer. It will
grow in wet mud, or very shallow water or in a moist
border. 75 × 30cm/2¹⁄₂ × 1ft

Ligularia przewalskii
Spires of golden flowers rise in mid to late summer
above mounds of bold jagged leaves. It is a vigorous
grower in rich, moist soil where it will make a
statuesque clump. 1.5 × 1m/5 × 3ft

***Lysichiton americanus* (Skunk cabbage)**
This has large yellow spathes in spring followed by big
cabbage-like leaves of bright green. It will grow in the
margins of a pool or in a moist or wet soil.
1.2 × 1m/4 × 3ft

Mimulus **'Orange Glow'**
There are many hybrids of the familiar monkey flower,
forming spreading carpets of colour with a long
flowering-season. They are mostly short-lived perennials
and not fully hardy. 20cm/8in H and W

Osmunda regalis **(Royal
fern)** LH
Splendid deciduous,
autumn-colouring fern for
moist, acid soil with erect
fronds up to 1.8m/6ft but
usually less. Prefers shade
but will usually stand full
sun in soil full of humus.
Usually 1.2m × 45cm/
4 × 1½ft

Lysichiton camtschatcensis
This lysichiton is a smaller version from the Orient with
white spathes in spring. Apart from its colour and size, it
is similar to its larger relative and has the same cultural
needs. 75 × 60cm/2½ × 2ft

185

Primula denticulata
(Drumstick primula)
A tough spring-flowering
primula with round
flowerheads of mauve or
white. 30cm/1ft H and W

Primula florindae **(Himalayan cowslip)**
A large imposing primula with clusters of pendent
yellow flowers in later summer. There is also a form with
flowers of a dusky red. 1m × 45cm/3 × 1¹⁄₂ft

Primula pulverulenta
An excellent candelabra
primula with tiers of
magenta blossoms in early
summer and mealy white
stems. The 'Bartley' form
has buff or pink flowers.
45 × 30cm/1¹⁄₂ × 1ft

***Primula* 'Valley Red'** ● ◐
A fine selected form of candelabra
primula which is a sound perennial and
looks dramatic when planted in mass. Its
richly coloured tiers of flowers bloom in
early summer. 30cm/1ft H and W

Primula vialii
A beautiful but short-lived species with
parti-coloured pokers of unopened red
flowers at the top and open lilac at the
bottom in summer. 30 × 20cm/1ft × 8in

Sinacalia tangutica (syn.
Senecio tanguticus)
A handsome perennial
with large conical heads of
small golden daisy flowers
in late summer to autumn
over jagged deeply cut
foliage. A spreader even in
clay soil. 1.5m × 60cm/
5 × 2ft

Rheum palmatum (Ornamental rhubarb)
A stunning foliage plant grown chiefly for its bold
deeply lobed foliage. In early summer, tall plumes of
white flowers, or red in the form 'Atrosanguineum', rise
above the leaves. 1.8 × 1m/6 × 3ft

CONSIDER ALSO:

Astilbe in variety p.161
Filipendula rubra p.21
Gentiana asclepiadea
  p.110
Hosta in variety
Lysimachia punctata
  p.23
Persicaria bistorta
  'Superba' p.105
Rodgersia in variety
  p.105
Telekia speciosa p.24

Trollius chinensis 'Golden Queen'
A beautiful marginal plant with orange
globular flowers in early summer. There
are many good globe flowers including
forms with pale creamy blooms.
60 × 30cm/2 × 1ft

Zantedeschia aethiopica 'Crowborough' ○
Fairly hardy arum lily flowering for a
long season, summer to autumn. A plant
for the moist border, but it will also grow
in shallow water. In either case, its tubers
should be protected from frost. 60cm/2ft
H and W

Ornamental Herbs

Give herbs an area to themselves because many self-sow
furiously. But if space is limited, some are ornamental
enough to merit a place in the border. All self-sowers will
need sharp watching; seed-heads should be removed and
seedlings which develop outside the allotted territory should
be dug up. Plant herbs in sun unless otherwise stated.

Bay (*Laurus nobilis*) E
A dark, aromatic-leafed evergreen shrub which lends
itself to topiary. Needs shelter in a harsh winter as it is
not fully hardy. Height according to pruning.

**Angelica (*Angelica
archangelica*)**
Decorative in leaf and
creamy flower. Perennial if
stopped from flowering.
Stems can be crystallized.
Self-sowing. 1.4m × 60cm/
5 × 2ft

Borage (*Borago officinalis*)
An annual with pretty, stamened, blue
flowers above coarse, hairy leaves.
Invasively self-sowing. 40 × 22cm/
1ft 4in × 9in

Chervil (*Anthriscus cerefolium*)
A self-sowing annual with dainty, feathery
leaves which will persist through the
winter if autumn sown. Useful for egg
dishes. 30 × 22cm/1ft × 9in

Chives (*Allium schoenoprasum*)
Useful edging plant with pink-purple flowers. The giant variety, *A.s. sibiricum,* is more decorative. Cut leaves from base to ensure a succession of shoots. 25 × 22cm/ 10 × 9in

Fennel (*Foeniculum vulgare*)
Feathery, green foliage but the bronze variety is more beautiful. Cut off golden flowerheads (unless seeds are for kitchen use) to prevent self-sowing and attain bushier plants. 1.2 × 1m/4 × 3ft

Hyssop (*Hyssopus officinalis*) E
Can be used in stews and salads but now grown chiefly as a useful evergreen sub-shrub with rich blue (or pink) flowers. 45cm/1½ft H and W

Marigold (*Calendula officinalis*)
An annual with a tradition as a border plant. Its orange-yellow petals can be used in salads. Invasively self-sowing. 45 × 30cm/1½ × 1ft

Lovage (*Levisticum officinale*)
A shapely plant with purple stems and glossy leaves which give a celery tang to stews. The stems can be crystallized when young and the seeds are sometimes used in baking. 1.2 × 1m/4 × 3ft

Marjoram
The variety *Origanum vulgare* 'Aureum' has golden leaves and dusty pink flowers.
30 × 45cm/1 × 1½ft

Mints can be decorative but their running rootstock can be very invasive if they are planted in a bed or border. It is more convenient if they are confined to a large pot or self-contained corner. There are two mints with especially pretty foliage.

Mentha × ***gentilis* 'Variegata' (Ginger mint)** ◖ (above)
Decorative gold and green mint which is also very invasive. Best grown in a container to curb its running tendencies. The leaf-tips are sometimes used in salads. 60cm/2ft × indefinite spread

Winter savory (*Satureja montana*) E
An evergreen sub-shrub with small mauve flowers. 30cm/1ft H and W

You can supplement this list with violas, pansies and nasturtiums whose flowers are edible. All these are possible front-of-border candidates. And don't forget rosemary (p.115), sage (p.115), golden balm (p.61) and thyme, of which the lemon, the caraway and the common thyme (*T. vulgaris*) are the best cooking varieties.

***Mentha suaveolens* 'Variegata' (Variegated apple mint)** ◖
A variegated cream and grey-green mint which is grown for its attractive summer foliage. 45 × 60cm/1½ × 2ft

Parsley (*Petroselinum crispum*)
An excellent edging plant or can be used in front-of-border groups in sun or shade. Biennial but sow annually for succession. 15cm/6in H and W

Trees, Hedges and Backgrounds

These are usually the dominant fundamentals in an area, partly because of their size. They are important for different reasons. Trees give height and shade to a garden, whereas hedges define its shape. Climbers are glamorous vertical furnishings, and large background features like pergolas or topiary give a garden a powerful individuality. The right choice and use of any of these plants or plant features is crucial because of their size and dominance.

Trees, Hedges and Backgrounds

Dominant plant features of this type should not usually be afterthoughts. They are the first fundamentals to which you add the smaller furnishings like beds and borders. If you are re-designing your whole garden or working on a blank canvas, here is your starting-point. If you simply want to add a hedge or a main feature to an existing garden, then be prepared for the possibility that it may dictate further changes.

The fact is that, even though such features may form backgrounds to other plants in the garden, they are part of its actual structure and therefore a key element in its design.

This is especially true of hedges. These are just as important as the partitions of a house, defining not only a room's extent, but its shape as well. They have a number of additional purposes to fulfil too. They give privacy, they screen unwanted views, they protect against intruders, and they give wind shelter also. They are actually far more effective against wind than solid walls, for they filter its force instead of blocking it and thereby causing undue turbulence and eddying.

The type of hedge you choose is an important decision. The possibilities are enormous, yet your requirements may narrow this array to a handful. You must decide whether you want it to be evergreen or deciduous; to flower, fruit or berry; to back a border, front a garden, or define a path. Do you want extreme formality or the irregularity of free growth? Would you like the type of hedge which is suited to incorporating 'windows' and 'doorways'? Do you want a circular or curving hedge? How often are you prepared to clip it and how much room do you have? On a more practical note, how much are you prepared to pay, for different varieties can vary greatly in price.

Whatever your choice, remember that it is likely to become a permanent feature in the garden; you will live with it for a long time.

A newly clipped hedge of copper beech.

Hedges: Preparation Planting and Aftercare

Planning is essential. The easiest way of choosing the site for a hedge is to test out its line in advance with string stretched along pegs. (Most hedges follow a straight line, but if you want a curved or circular hedge, use a centrally placed batten and attach to it a string lead which can be swivelled in an arc.) Then, visualize how the fully-grown hedge will look in this position; or, alternatively, take a photograph of the area and draw in the hedge on the print. When planning the site, take into account any eyesores that should be screened. Consider, too, where you need your openings and, if there is to be more than one aperture, are they lined up if necessary? Finally, make sure that you allow room for the hedge's thickness; as much as 1m/3ft from the nearest plants in a border, and not less than 60cm/2ft distance from a path.

CALCULATING THE NUMBER OF PLANTS

This estimate will depend on the intervals required between the plants. Remember that the first and last plants don't go in at the very end of a row, but at a distance of half the usual interval, to allow for their eventual spread. The number of plants will also vary (obviously) if you plant a double row (or even treble) of staggered plants with the purpose of making an extra-strong barrier.

DIGGING THE SOIL

When you have decided on the site, kill off all perennial weeds in the area with a weed-killer that does not poison the soil. Then, dig a trench along the line of string and pegs to a spade's depth and about 1m/3ft width for a single row of plants. (Increase this width to 1.5m/5ft if you will be planting a double row.) If the soil is seriously waterlogged, the soil must be dug to double the spade's depth and, without bringing the lower spit of subsoil to the upper spit, insert plastic drainage pipes and rubble. Otherwise, the hedge will simply perish. To give any hedge a good start, work old dung, compost or fertilizer into the trench but cover this with good topsoil so that the hedge's roots are not in direct contact with it.

PLANTING

You can plant deciduous hedges any time between autumn and spring so long as the soil isn't frozen or sticky with rain. Plant evergreens in early autumn or mid-late spring when the soil is warmer. In a cold or exposed spot, evergreens will also need some protection against icy, scourging winds, to prevent them suffering from wind-burn which can be fatal. In this case, erect in advance polythene sheeting (supported on stakes) on the wind-exposed side of the planting line.

To ensure you plant your hedge in an absolutely straight (or perfectly curved) line, make an indentation in the earth or nick out the soil to a spade's depth immediately below the taut string you have stretched on pegs. Keeping accurately to this indentation, plant each shrub to the depth of its original soil line, having spread out the roots on bare-rooted plants. Put the finest soil around the roots before filling in the rest of the hole with earth. Firm down the soil around each plant to prevent it suffering from wind-rock. Tall, thin plants may need to be tied to a stake and, in this case, the pole should be fixed stoutly in the planting hole in advance.

WATERING AND MULCHING

The young hedge will have to be kept watered in dry weather, and this is especially important for evergreens which can die in a spring drought. Mulch the hedge also to conserve moisture.

CLIPPING

The most suitable pruning time/s for each variety of hedge are given in the description for each individual shrub. But as a general principle, those that need hard clipping in their early years to induce lush growth at the base can be cut back in the spring of the following year if they are spring planted, or 18 months after autumn planting. Otherwise, let the leader or growing shoot continue until the desired height is reached, but trim the side shoots regularly.

Always make sure that the base of the hedge is broader and bushier than the top. This produces a sloping effect which is called a batter. It allows light and air to reach the lower branches which encourages strong growth; it prevents gappiness at the base; it results in greater stability.

Hedges lend themselves also to a variety of decorative treatments. You can give them 'doors' and 'windows'; you can top them with topiary; you can trim them to form stilt hedges which look like slim, green boxes on poles.

FEEDING

All trimmed hedges respond to being fed, for severe clipping makes demands on the shrubs. To keep them in peak condition, give them old manure or compost, bonemeal or liquid manure in the spring.

Evergreen Hedges

Tall, dense, evergreen hedges are virtually living walls and can be used as such. At all times of the year, they form barriers within a garden and redoubtable boundaries around it. Some of those listed below are far too big for small gardens, as they will outgrow their station on reaching maturity. Others, however, can be kept clipped into slimness and should be preferred where space is short. Some flower and fruit, others give a more self-effacing display but lend themselves to intricate trimming to provide doorways, windows and topiary shapes. Quick-growing varieties are more demanding, as they require clipping three or even four times a year. The slow hedges make you wait, but repay this disadvantage by needing only one annual clip. Varieties with very large leaves look best if they are hand-trimmed with secateurs to avoid mutilating their foliage, and in such cases, the length of hedge should be taken into account. A few varieties are toxic to stock and should not be grown where animals can reach the leaves.

Aucuba japonica E
Handsome hedge especially in the variegated form or berrying (female) clones. Tolerant of poor soil and shade. Large leaves need careful trimming with secateurs. Plant 1m/3ft apart. 2.4m/8ft

Berberis × *stenophylla* E
Vigorous, dark, dense hedge with an arching habit of growth. Its thorns help to keep out intruders. Gold flowers in early spring. Plant 45cm/1½ft apart. Clip after flowering. 2.4m/8ft

Buxus sempervirens **'Handsworthensis'** E **(Box)**
Makes a dark formal hedge up to 4m/13ft with aromatic leaves. Needs well-drained soil and is good on chalk. Plant 45cm/1½ft apart. Trim in early summer and again, if needed, in early autumn.

Chamaecyparis lawsoniana **(Lawson cypress)** E
Coniferous hedge which is good in wind and part-shade. There are many cultivars of different shades from blue to bright green to gold. Normal rate of growth is about 60cm/2ft a year, but 'Ellwoodii' (above), with grey-green foliage, steel blue in winter, is a much slower cultivar, reducing the need to clip. Plant about 1m/3ft apart.

Cotoneaster franchetii var. **sternianus** E
A beautiful hedge which can be kept slim, bearing white flowers in spring and coral berries. Sage-green leaves with a silver underside. Plant 45cm/1½ft apart. Trim after growth has finished. 2.4m/8ft

Cotoneaster lacteus
This cotoneaster is vigorous and fast-growing with long-lasting red berries that follow on from its small white flowers. It is tolerant of most soils. Plant 45cm/1½ft apart. 2.4m/8ft

× **Cupressocyparis leylandii** (**Leyland cypress**) E
Another coniferous hedge with phenomenally speedy growth needing at least three trims a year. It soon outgrows its station. Plant 1m/3ft apart.

× **Cupressocyparis leylandii** 'Castlewellan' E
This popular golden form of Leyland cypress is sometimes called 'Galway Gold'. It does not grow quite so quickly as the green form.

Olearia macrodonta E
A reasonably hardy shrub
with holly-like leaves, sage-
green above and silvery
beneath, and a profuse
display of white daisy
flowers in summer. Best on
acid soil. Plant in spring
1m/3ft apart. Clip after
flowering 2.1m/7ft

Pyracantha in variety
(**Firethorn**) E
This tough shrub with its
white flowers in spring
followed by a display of
berries makes a handsome
hedge especially if yellow
and red fruited varieties
are mixed. 3m/10ft

Ilex (**Holly**) E
Many hollies make excellent hedges in sun or shade and on any soil. *Ilex × altaclarensis*
'Camelliifolia' is dark green and almost spineless. At the other extreme is *Ilex
aquifolium* 'Ferox Argentea', (shown here) the silver hedgehog holly, with spines on the
upperside as well as around its leaves. Margins and spines are creamy-white. Plant
about 45–60cm/1½–2ft apart. Ultimate height around 8m/26ft if required.

Prunus laurocerasus (**Laurel**) E
This makes an attractive bright hedge with its glossy
emerald foliage but can look ugly after clipping if its
large leaves have been cut in two by the machine. Plant
1m/3ft apart. 3m/10ft

Taxus baccata (Yew) E
A superb hedge which is tolerant of most soils except those that are waterlogged. It grows about 30cm/1ft a year and is clipped in late summer. Ideal for arches or topiary trimmings. Plant 60cm–1m/2–3ft apart. 5m/16ft

Thuja plicata E
The western red cedar is a fast-growing hedge needing two clips, but is suited to a narrow space as it can be kept slim. Plant 60cm/2ft apart. 3m/10ft or more. *T. occidentalis* is a slowish-growing conifer thriving in any well-drained soil with many cultivars of green or gold. Needs clipping only once a year.

Tapestry hedges
Hedges can be made out of a variety of plants. The secret of a successful tapestry hedge is to combine plants whose habits and rates of growth are similar. The effect is particularly dramatic when the hedge design emphasises the different plants as here where gold and green conifers form a battlemented combination.

This tapestry hedge combines deciduous as well as evergreen plants. The effect is wonderful but needs careful management to ensure that the stronger-growing inmates do not take over the weaker.

Formally Clipped Deciduous Hedges

A formally clipped deciduous hedge will form as effective a barrier or background when in leaf as any evergreen hedge, but in winter most varieties will be see-through. An exception to this is beech (*Fagus*) which retains its dead leaves, and also, to a lesser extent, hornbeam (*Carpinus*).

Carpinus betulus (Hornbeam)
A strong, dense hedge resembling beech, to which it is far superior on heavy, wet soils. It retains its withered donkey-brown leaves throughout the winter if clipped in late summer. Plant 45–60cm/1½–2ft apart. Up to 5m/16ft if necessary.

***Crataegus monogyna* (Hawthorn)**
Not for formal surroundings, but makes a good, cheap, clipped hedge in the country. Thorny, tough, tolerant of any soil and adaptable to topiary. White flowers in late spring and dark red fruit in autumn. Plant 30cm/1ft apart and trim in late autumn. 4m/13ft

Fagus sylvatica (Beech)
Probably the best formal, deciduous hedge and good on all well-drained soils. Its leaves turn russet in autumn and, if pruned in late summer, will remain throughout the winter. Good topiary subject. Plant 45–60cm/1½–2ft apart and don't trim the leaders until the desired height is reached.

Prunus cerasifera 'Pissardii' (or 'Nigra')
A small tree which can be grown as a vigorous, bushy hedge. At its finest in spring when starred with pale pink flowers, but its foliage, first ruby then deepening to black-purple, is a useful contrast to a pale border near it. Unfortunately it needs clipping three times a year and needs careful siting for maximum convenience. Plant 75cm/2½ft apart. 3.5m/12ft

Flowering Hedges

Another category of hedge which can make an ornamental screen or division is the deciduous hedge formed of attractive flowering shrubs. Its effect is at the opposite extreme from the dark and severe architecture of most formal boundary or border hedges. Many of the varieties are allowed to grow fairly freely, or, if pruned, given only a slight trim rather than carved into a rectangular block. The tougher, larger varieties will make powerful windbreaks. The more floriferous and ornamental are better treated as garden features in their own right, perhaps, for example, bordering a grass walk where they serve to replace a border, being spreading, linear and colourful. Some are even sometimes used as boundary shrubs around a front garden but, being deciduous, provide inadequate cover in winter. But, wherever they are placed, nearly all these colour hedges need siting with care. The massed colours of some flowers can be overpowering and even offensive if placed near hot competition.

Chaenomeles × superba
'Crimson and Gold'
(Japonica)
This spreading shrub makes a fine bright hedge in spring when it flowers, after which it can be clipped. Here it is grown against a railing which gives extra support. The form 'Rowallane' also makes a good hedge. Plant 60cm/2ft apart. 1.2m/4ft

Hydrangea arborescens
'Grandiflora' ◑
A loose shrub which bears great domes of greenish-white flowers in summer through till autumn. It is inclined to loll and is best against support like a low wall. Plant 60cm–1m/2–3ft apart and trim in early spring. 1m/3ft

Fuchsia **'Riccartonii'**
This fuchsia is the hardiest of all varieties, making a beautiful informal hedge in sheltered gardens. Plant 45cm/1½ft apart and trim in early spring if necessary. 1.2m/4ft

FLOWERING HEDGES

Certain groups of shrub roses make the most beautiful of all deciduous flowering hedges though they must be encouraged to become bushy at the base before developing. Cut them back hard in the spring following planting. Thereafter prune lightly, but remove weak or dead growth.

Rosa 'Roseraie de l'Haÿ' ○
One of the best examples from the Rugosa rose group. It bears very fragrant, velvety, purplish-crimson large flowers with golden stamens recurrently from early summer till autumn. Plant 1m/3ft apart. 1.8m/6ft. 'Scabrosa' with single magenta flowers and large hips is also suitable. 1.5m/5ft

Rosa 'Penelope' ○
This creamy-pink hybrid musk rose which is very scented makes a good healthy hedge. It flowers for a long period from early summer onwards. 1.8m/6ft

Rosa 'Queen Elizabeth' ○
This floribunda, or cluster-flowered, rose is a popular hedging choice. It blooms continuously and is strong and vigorous. 1.5m/5ft

Rosa mundi (*Rosa gallica versicolor*) ○
An old French (Gallica) rose that has bright green
foliage and very fragrant pink cerise-striped flowers. It
makes a wonderful once-flowering low hedge. 1.2m/4ft

CONSIDER ALSO:
Rosa glauca p.91

Viburnum opulus 'Sterile'
(Snowball bush)
This forms a much more
showy hedge with large
white globular flowerheads
in early summer. It is
infertile, so no fruit
follows. Its leaves colour
well in autumn. 2.4m/8ft

Viburnum opulus (Guelder rose)
This makes a pretty informal hedge for wilder areas with white lacecap flowers in
early summer followed by red berries in autumn. The yellow berried form *V. o.*
'Xanthocarpum' is an attractive variant. 2.4m/8ft

Hedging Shrubs for Seaside

Shrubs need to be tolerant of wind and sometimes even of salt spray if they are planted near the sea. However, one advantage of this position is that the winter frosts are not so severe with the result that shrubs that are doubtfully hardy can thrive.

Escallonia 'Apple Blossom' E: ○
Glossy green leaves and pink and white flowers in summer make this an attractive option. Escallonias withstand wind and salt spray. 1.8m/6ft

Griselinia littoralis E
Establish in spring on a well-drained site for it is not ideally suited to cold areas. It is good on chalk. Glossy apple-green leaves, handsome in the plain or cream-variegated forms. Plant 1m/3ft apart. Prune in spring. 2.4m/8ft

Tamarix tetrandra (Tamarisk) ○
Soft feathery glaucous scale-like foliage makes this a graceful shrub at all seasons. In early summer it becomes plumed with long clusters of tiny pink flowers. Prune after flowering. It withstands salt winds. 4m/13ft

CONSIDER ALSO:

Escallonia 'Iveyi' p.179
Fuchsia magellanica
Hebe × franciscana
 'Blue Gem'
Hydrangea macrophylla
Olearia macrodonta
 p.198

Garrya elliptica E
A Californian shrub making a marvellous hedge in sheltered positions, with glaucous leaves and silvery catkins in late winter. The female's catkins are much shorter, so ensure you buy the male plant, the best clone of which is called 'James Roof'. Plant 1m/3ft apart. Prune in spring. 2.1m/7ft

Low Dividers

CONSIDER ALSO:

Hyssopus officinalis
  p.189
Salvia officinalis p.115
Rosmarinus officinalis
  'Miss Jessop's
  Upright' (syn.
  'Fastigiatus') p.115

All low dividers are only for use in cultivated areas, otherwise infiltrating weeds will soon overpower them. They vary in height from a few inches to 1.2m/4ft. They cannot be used for screening, but are excellent for edges, to provide a frame, or even a pattern within whose outline different plants can be grown (on the model of the old knot gardens).

Cotoneaster horizontalis
The fish-bone cotoneaster can make an unusual informal low hedge with a spraying habit if it is grown against a support which it can drape over. 75cm/2½ft

***Buxus sempervirens* 'Suffruticosa'** E
The edging box which can be kept clipped to a few centimetres. Plant 15cm/6in apart and trim in early summer, and again if needed in autumn. 30cm/1ft

***Fagus sylvatica* 'Atropurpurea' (Purple-leafed beech)**
A lovely hedge with glossy dark leaves which would form an excellent backdrop to a red border. 1m/3ft upwards

Ligustrum ovalifolium
'Aureum' (Golden privet)
Semi-E
This small-leafed shrub
will require trimming
several times a year to
keep it low and compact.
Its gold foliage makes a
bright cheerful hedge.
Height as required.

Lavandula in variety (**Lavender**) E: ○
L. angustifolia 'Hidcote' will make a low dense aromatic
hedge of grey foliage with violet flowers in summer.
45cm/1½ft. 'Grappenhall', Dutch lavender with paler
purple spikes, will reach 1.2m/4ft in flower.

Lonicera nitida E
A tiny-leafed evergreen which grows fast and will
therefore require several clips a year to keep it neat and
dense. 60cm–1.5m/2–5ft

Santolina chamaecyparissus (**Cotton lavender**) E: ○
This makes a low dense hedge of pale grey foliage
that withstands clipping well. Cut before the yellow
bobble flowers are produced in summer. 45cm/1½ft

Hedges for Borders

Any hedge which is used to back a border should be a variety which lends itself to formal clipping. Other factors matter too. Its roots should not be unduly invasive and greedy. Its width is important: a slim border needs a slim hedge; a larger border can share its space with a corpulent hedge like yew. Colour can be another consideration, for the purple-leafed varieties are sometimes used to provide a contrast to pale flowers before them. One practical factor is especially important; as a general rule, confine yourself to those hedges which need only one annual clip. It is a major drawback not only to prune but pick up the fallen twigs at the back of a border more than once a year.

This elegant treatment of a narrow border backed by a hedge shows how effective the simple contrast of vertical and horizontal lines can be. The globular heads of the ornamental onion, *Allium aflatunense*, break up the straight lines of the box hedge in front and the full-size backing hedge.

A yew hedge with an arch forms the background to a foam of herbaceous plants, including the white *Epilobium angustifolium album* which shines out againt the darkness of the yew behind.

Pleached Alleys

Pleached alleys form a similar galleried walk to pergolas, but their actual structure differs in that it is formed from trees or large shrubs trained over strong wires, iron hoops or timber frames so that the tops of the plants interlace. Hawthorn was a favourite medieval subject; hornbeam, elm and lime attained later popularity; yew was favoured for the darkest of evergreen tunnels. In this century, laburnum has been a first choice to make this formal type of passage, its golden racemes weeping down within the framework in early summer. But hooped cordons of apple trees are almost as lovely in blossom, and also decorative when fruiting.

The simplest form of topiary is the stilt hedge. For this purpose, standard hornbeams or limes with clear stems to 1.8m/6ft are usually planted – firmly staked with a strong bamboo tied to the stake, extending the vertical line. Three or four stout horizontal bamboos are lashed to that and the trees branches trained to these lines.

The idea of a tunnel made of golden laburnums has become very popular in recent years. Its great advantage is that it is showy, quick-growing and easily trained. The commonly planted form which has long flower-chains is *Laburnum × watereri* 'Vossii'. All parts are poisonous.

Topiary

Nothing can equal topiary in making a garden memorable and individual, yet this living sculpture can be designed and executed without difficulty. The choice of design, however, needs thought, for it can make a garden dramatic, dignified or absurd.

Very hardy evergreens with smallish leaves and a dense habit of growth are best and will ease the gardener's lot if the plants grow slowly enough to require no more than an annual clip.

The ideal subject is *Taxus baccata* (yew, below left) but *Buxus* (box, below right) is almost as good, even for intricate shapes.

Consider also *Laurus nobilis* (bay laurel) in mild areas, *Prunus lusitanica* (Portugal laurel), pyracantha, *Ilex* (holly) and *Viburnum tinus* for simple shapes.

Deciduous plants like *Fagus* (beech), *Carpinus* (hornbeam) and *Crataegus* × *monogyna* (hawthorn) can be trained to form useful doorways and apertures in a hedge.

Training topiary shapes
To make a design, allow the shoots of the plant to grow on until they are long enough to train. You can tie them with tarred string to a bamboo or a wire framework which will form the design. Alternatively, you could make a light wooden frame of lattice-work and the small plant's new growth can be trimmed close to the frame. Clip the trained shrub or tree at the season suggested in the text describing the plant, or in late summer if not specified.

You can use either hand or electric shears for small-leafed subjects like yew and box, but secateurs are preferable for larger-leafed plants such as holly or bay whose leaves would be spoilt without individual attention. Don't clip for at least a year after planting and never clip if the branch can be trained into the shrub. Any clipping makes demands on the plant and it will need to be fed in spring with old manure or compost, bonemeal or liquid manure to keep it in peak condition.

Doorways

Although not necessarily ornamental in themselves, doorways are admirable tools of design in a hedged enclosure, if two can be lined up to afford a beautiful through-view. The easiest way to make a doorway is to bend over growths from the plants either side of the aperture you have left in the planting line, until they join hands, lashing them if necessary to a horizontal bamboo.

Windows

Hedge windows are not so commonly seen, but can be a valuable frame to a fine view. They need to be trained from the beginning by pinching out new growths around the intended inner frame. Early training avoids the risks attached to cutting into the main wood which might be unavoidable if you decide to hack out a window when the hedge is mature.

Plants for the Foot of Hedges

Hedges tend to be greedy-rooted creatures and the soil immediately around them is almost certain to be dry and robbed of nutrients. In a large border beside a hedge, you can leave a space between the plants and the bottom of the hedge, but where the area is only several feet, you have little option if you wish to plant it but must confine your choice to those tough, surface-rooting subjects which will tolerate poor conditions. In sun, the most suitable plants are those which enjoy a summer baking but winter shelter, and these include a number of small bulbs. In shade, only those plants which will thrive in dry shade are possibilities.

The hedge bottom must be weed-free before you establish any of the plants. Even though most are tough survivors, it is too much to expect them to cope with hedge roots *and* weeds.

Allium moly
Rather invasive, small ornamental onion with glaucous leaves and golden flowers in summer. For sun or shade. Many other small alliums are also suitable in sun, including the pink, *A. ostrowskianum*. Both 20cm/8in

Narcissi and **daffodils**
The stronger growing cultivars are particularly useful in front of a dark evergreen hedge such as yew here. Suitable forms might include 'Ice Follies', a white narcissus with a pale lemon cup fading to white; or the yellow daffodil 'Golden Harvest'. 45cm/1½ft or less

***Ornithogalum umbellatum*
(Star of Bethlehem)**
A small bulb with grassy
leaves and starry white
flowers in late spring. It
will spread happily along
the bottom of a hedge.
20cm/8in

Species tulips ○
Graceful bulbs most of which need a
summer baking to thrive. If their position
is hot and well drained, they can be left
to naturalize. Suitable varieties include
Tulipa sprengeri (above), the last tulip to
flower, in early summer and worth
waiting for. Its scarlet flowers, buff on the
outside, look very handsome in front of a
dark leafed hedge like purple beech or
prunus. It will also tolerate part-shade.
45cm/1½ft

Other suitable varieties
of tulip include the
yellow *T. sylvestris* and
T. tarda, a good
naturalizer.

Anthemis punctata subsp. *cupaniana* E: ○
White daisy flowers most of the summer over mounds of
cut silver leaves. Makes a rampant carpeter but must
have full sun. 30 × 45cm/1 × 1½ft

Aquilegia vulgaris (**Columbine**)
The wild aquilegia has pendent flowers in early
summer which are usually purple but can be white or
pink. It will self-seed happily. 60 × 30cm/2 × 1ft

Dryopteris filix-mas (**Male fern**) ◑ ●
A handsome deciduous fern which forms the shape of a
shuttlecock as it matures. A strong grower in shade. It
prefers moist soil but will tolerate dry. 1.2 × 1m/4 × 3ft

Galium odoratum
The sweet woodruff is spreading and tolerant of dry
shade. White starry flower heads in early summer with
the scent of new-mown hay. 15 × 30cm/6in × 1ft

Euphorbia robbiae E
Very spreading but
handsome shrubby
perennial with dark
evergreen rosettes of
leaves and, in spring to
early summer, sprays of
lime-green bracts rising to
60cm/2ft. Sun or shade.
Plant 30cm/1ft apart, but
the spread is indefinite.

Geranium pratense (Meadow cranesbill)
Native plant with violet-blue flowers in early summer
and leaves colouring well in autumn. Lusty spreader
and self-sowing. 60/2ft H and W

***Hebe pinguifolia* 'Pagei'** E:○
A prostrate shrub with tiny blue-grey evergreen leaves
and white flowers in early summer, making excellent
ground-cover. 15 × 45cm/6in × 1½ft

Lamium maculatum E: ◖
Forms a spreading carpet
of green-margined, silver-
splashed foliage with pink
flowers in early to mid-
summer. 10 × 40cm/
4in × 1ft 4in. (See also *L.
galeobdolon* 'Florentinum'
on page 113.)

***Lunaria annua* 'Alba Variegata' (Honesty)**
A biennial but self-sowing. The white variegated form of
honesty with cream-splashed leaves and flowers in early
summer, followed by silvery, papery seed-heads.
75 × 30cm/2½ × 1ft

Meconopsis cambrica
Invasively self-sowing but delicately pretty yellow or orange summer-flowering Welsh poppy. Both single and double forms exist, though the latter can only be propagated by division. Sun or shade. 30 x 22cm/ 1ft × 9in

Myrrhis odorata (**Sweet Cicely**)
The ferny leaves of this herb appear early in the year and die back late. Small white flowers appear in summer. It will self-sow unless these are cut off before going to seed. 60cm/2ft H and W

Osteospermum jucundum (**African daisy**) ○
Dark-eyed, lilac-pink daisy flowers with grey-blue undersides produced over many months from early summer onwards. Makes spreading mats of narrow leaves. Not reliably hardy and needs full sun. Up to 30cm/1ft H and W

Phuopsis stylosa (syn. *Crucianella stylosa*) ◯
Small rounded heads of minute pink flowers in early
summer above narrow, pointed leaves, forming a mat.
20 × 45cm/8in × 1¹/₂ft

Pentaglottis sempervirens **(Alkanet)**
The bright azure flowers in late spring of this wild
perennial with its coarse leaves are suitable in front of
an informal hedge. 75 × 30cm/2¹/₂ × 1ft

Persicaria campanulata
A spreading, shallow-rooting plant with pale pink,
sweet-scented flower heads produced over a long season
from summer to autumn. Sun or shade. 75 × 60cm/
2¹/₂ × 2ft

Polygonatum × hybridum (Solomon's seal)
Graceful, arching stems bearing fresh green, ribbed leaves and small white pendulous flowers in late spring to early summer. Spreading rootstock, even in dry shade. 75 × 30cm/2½ × 1ft

Tanacetum vulgare (Tansy)
A somewhat invasive but useful flowering herb with very decorative leaves and yellow blooms in summer. 75cm/2½ft H and W

Vinca minor 'Burgundy' E: ◑ ●
This distinctively coloured form of the lesser periwinkle with small dark green leaves will make near-prostrate groundcover in shady conditions. It blooms in spring but a sprinkling of flowers continues till autumn. The soil should not be too dry.
15 × 60cm/6in × 2ft

PLANTS FOR THE FOOT OF HEDGES: PERENNIALS AND LOW SHRUBS

Screens

Screening shrubs and trees are usually planted for one of three purposes: to hide an eyesore; to act as a windbreak; or to give privacy to a garden. Plants required for the first purpose should be evergreen and ornamental – bamboos are excellent subjects, though even they tend to look tatty in a hard winter. Taller eyesores can be effectively blocked with grouped conifers, not in a line but staggered.

For use as a windbreak, trees can be evergreen or deciduous, but must be thoroughly hardy inland or, if by the sea, able to endure salt gales. Many are ultimately large and quite unsuited to the smaller garden, though the *Crataegus* species and cotoneaster are useful here, as are the hollies (*Ilex*) mentioned on pages 65 and 198. Screens planted for privacy are best selected from the evergreens listed below or under Evergreen Hedges (pages 196–9). If the latter, planting distances must be increased.

BAMBOOS

Fargesia (syn. *Arundinaria*) ***nitida*** E
A most decorative clump-former with narrow green leaves on arching canes giving a very dainty appearance, especially when frosted, as shown here. Needs protection from wind. 4m/13ft

Pseudosasa (syn. *Arundinaria*) ***japonica*** E: ◑
A common, very hardy bamboo tolerating windswept positions. It makes a dense screen to 4.5m/15ft, with deep green canes and leaves up to 30cm/1ft long, rich green above, part grey below. Spreads by rhizomes and sometimes invasive. Better in part-shade.

USEFUL SCREENING SHRUBS

Rhododendron ponticum E: LH: ◑
The common rhododendron with mauve flowers in late spring. It needs acid soil and self-sows and layers where suited. Bushy and spreading. Toxic to stock. Plant 1m/3ft apart. 3m/10ft

Viburnum tinus E
A shrub with dark, shiny leaves and pinkish-white flower clusters in winter. Plant 60cm/2ft apart and trim after flowering is finished in spring. 3m/10ft

***Crataegus* species**
Many thorn-trees are ornamental and all are tough, bushy-headed, tolerant of any soil and situation and suitable for small gardens. *C × prunifolia* has dark, glossy green leaves turning red in autumn when it also bears dark red fruit. 5m/16ft

Quercus cerris
The Turkey oak is slender and open when young, domed when old and has dark green leaves. Good in maritime exposure rather than inland. Very rapid growth to 35m/116ft and only for large gardens.

CONSIDER ALSO:
Acer pseudoplatanus
   p.236
Alnus glutinosa
Cotoneaster × watereri
Populus alba
P. tremula
P. 'Robusta'

EVERGREEN WINDBREAK TREES

***Pinus nigra* E**
The dense, burly Austrian pine with very dark stiff needles and cones up to 7.5cm/3in long. First-class windbreak. Good even in chalky soil, but it is only suited to large gardens. 30m/100ft

***Pinus radiata* E: LH**
The rapid-growing Monterey pine with bright green needles up to 15cm/6in long and cones up to 12cm/5in. Picturesque but generally better suited to milder, large gardens only. 30m/100ft

Climbers

Climbing plants support themselves, whether by aerial roots or by adhesive pads or by twining stems (or leaf stems) or by spines on their long arching shoots which hook into and over objects in their path. Others are not strictly speaking climbers, but will shove and lean their way up a wall, or can be trained by securing their stems to wires or trellis. All these different types are indispensable for hiding unsightly boundaries or buildings, whether walls, fences, screens or sheds. Festoon these eyesores with colour and foliage, and you have a vertical garden instead. Climbers are also key plants for providing privacy, and if they are grown against a trellis or netting erected above a low wall, they will give a high degree of seclusion. Plan their position carefully, relating their ultimate height and vigour of growth to the situation they will occupy. This is important, because it is not so simple to rid yourself of a mistake when the plant has covered the wall.

Clematis armandii E: ○
Trifoliate leaves and scented flowers in spring which are white in the form 'Snowdrift' and blush in the cultivar 'Apple Blossom'. Vigorous to 4m/13ft but a sheltered, sunny wall is essential. Provide support.

Fremontodendron **'Californian Glory'** E: ○
A fast-growing plant with beautiful golden cupped flowers produced from spring through until autumn. Its lobed leaves are felted beneath with rusty down. Not a climber but best placed against a sunny wall. Not fully hardy. 5m/16ft

Hedera colchica 'Sulphur Heart' (Ivy) E
A large-leafed handsome form with a golden central
splash to the leaf. It is self-clinging and suitable for
growing on a wall but, as with all ivies, it is sensible to
ensure that the wall is sound and cannot be damaged by
the ivy. 4.5m/15ft

**Trachelospermum
asiaticum** E: ○
A dense, self-clinging
climber with evergreen
leaves and creamy,
fragrant, jasmine-like
flowers in later summer.
Needs a warm wall. Rather
slow. 6m/20ft

Lonicera japonica 'Halliana' (Honeysuckle) E or semi-E
A rampant climber with fragrant white, ageing to yellow,
flowers from summer to autumn. It needs support and
firm pruning. 10m/33ft

CLIMBERS: LARGE-FLOWERED CLEMATIS

Clematis are an immensely varied group, all of which need their roots shaded to thrive. Plant the root ball 5cm/2½in deeper than the soil level in the pot to protect against wilt, and tie stems to wall support.

C. 'Ernest Markham'
A valuable climber which has carmine flowers and yellow anthers in late summer. It is a very vigorous hybrid. 3–4m/10–13ft

C. 'Perle d'Azur'
A late-flowering variety which bears azure blue blooms from summer to early autumn. 3–4m/10–13ft

See also *C.* 'Jackmanii Superba' on p. 148.

C. 'Nelly Moser'
This popular form gives a prolific display of pale mauve flowers with a deeper bar in early summer and a secondary show in late summer. 3–4m/10–13ft

C. 'Marie Boisselot' (syn. 'Madame le Coultre')
A dazzling clematis bearing very large white flowers with yellow anthers from summer onwards. It will grow vigorously in sun or shade. 3–4m/10–13ft

C. alpina
Early spring-flowering, blue in the type, though there is
a purplish-pink form shown here, called 'Ruby' and a
double white cultivar ('White Moth'). 3m/10ft

C. montana rubens
This very vigorous plant
flowers in late spring,
growing to 10m/33ft. The
white form, *C. montana*, is
equally rampant.

C. macropetala
This species blooms in spring. The blue 'Maidwell Hall'
is shown here. It looks at its prettiest beside the pink
cultivar 'Markham's Pink', also shown. 3m/10ft

C.m. 'Tetrarose'
This montana clematis is
less vigorous and bears
rosy-lilac flowers and
bronzed foliage.

225

CLIMBERS: CLEMATIS SPECIES

The late-flowering species clematis are both beautiful and useful, prolonging the season of colour. They are usually hard pruned in late winter or earliest spring and will make vigorous growth in the next few months to flower from the second half of the summer into autumn.

See also *Clematis cirrhosa balearica* on p.138 and *Clematis armandii* p.222.

***Clematis orientalis* (Orange-peel clematis)**
A late-flowering species with thickly textured lantern-shaped yellow sepals and fluffy silvery seed-heads. 'Bill MacKenzie' is a good form and more vigorous than the type. 4m/13ft

Clematis tangutica
A late-flowering species with nodding yellow bells which are followed by silky silvery seed-heads, attractive in their own right. Vigorous to 5m/16ft

C. viticella
The viticella clematis bloom in summer to autumn. The deepest purple form is 'Royal Velours', shown here growing over a pink *Lavatera*. There is also a white, green-tipped form called 'Alba Luxurians'. 'Rubra' with wine-red flowers is equally good. 3m/10ft

***C. viticella* 'Purpurea Plena Elegans'**
A double viticella clematis which bears a large number of blooms over a long period. 3m/10ft

Of the easily
obtainable cultivars,
the roses shown here
are fine
representatives of the
different colour
ranges. Tie all to
supports on a wall.

R. 'Guinée' ○
A very velvety deep red rose, almost
black as a bud, with a powerful scent. A
vigorous climber but only once flowering.
6m/20ft

R. 'Lady Waterlow'
A climbing rose of the hybrid tea type
with lovely lightly scented flowers
produced freely in early summer, with a
second scattering in late summer.
3.5m/12ft

**R. 'Mme. Grégoire
Staechelin'**
Once-blooming only in
early summer but has an
impressive display of large,
scented pink flowers,
crimson in bud. Large hips
follow. 7m/23ft

R. 'Mermaid' ○
Loveliest of the yellows
with large, single flowers
all summer and semi-
evergreen leaves. Needs
ample space and a
sheltered wall. Do not
prune. 9m/30ft

R. 'Mme. Alfred Carrière'
A sweetly scented and
perpetual flowering rose
with double blush-white
flowers and disease-free
foliage. Also good for
north walls. 6m/20ft

R. 'New Dawn'
This apple-scented rose
has recurrent-flowering,
flesh-pink blooms and
dark, glossy leaves which
are very healthy. 4m/13ft

Consider also the rapid
climbers shown on
page 150: *Cobaea
scandens, Ipomoea,
Lathyrus odoratus,*
Nasturtium, *Thunbergia
alata*

Actinidia kolomikta ○
Slow to start, but very striking when established on a
sunny wall, this climber's leaves are often part-pink or
white. 4m/13ft

Akebia quinata Semi-E: ○
A vigorous and unusual climber with dusky purple
vanilla-scented flowers in late spring followed by
purplish brown sausages. Light-green foliage. For a
warm position. 9m/10ft

Passiflora caerulea Semi-E:
○
The beautiful and
rampant, blue and white-
flowered passion flower,
blossoming in summer-
autumn, when it produces
orange fruits. There is a
fine white form called
'Constance Elliot'. 6m/20ft

***Campsis × tagliabuana* 'Madame Galen'** ○
A very vigorous climber which needs support. Pinnate
leaves and showy trumpet flowers in late summer. Full
sun is essential for a wonderful plant giving brilliant
colour late in the year. To 6m/20ft

***Solanum crispum* 'Glasnevin'** semi-E: ○
Lanky but rapid grower with semi-evergreen leaves
and violet flowers with a yellow staminal beak, borne
in clusters all summer. Give it firm support against a
wall. 5m/16ft

Vitis coignetiae ○
A rampant, ornamental vine with big
leaves, turning crimson in autumn in the
best forms. Give it plenty of space for it
will cover a high house wall, given
support. Ultimately up to 20m/66ft

***Vitis vinifera* 'Purpurea'** ○
The black grapes of this vine are inedible
and it is grown only for its foliage. The
new olive green leaves turn dark red,
then purple. 4m/13ft

Wisteria floribunda ○
Arguably the noblest of all climbers with 60cm/2ft
long trusses of scented pea-flowers. In the form
'Macrobotrys' they reach 1m/3ft long but the upper
flowers tend to have died off before the lower ones
open. 5m/16ft

Wisteria sinensis ○
This lovely climber is a very vigorous grower with
mauve flowers in early summer. White and pink forms
are obtainable also, and there is a double purple variety
called 'Black Dragon'. The flowering racemes are about
25cm/10in long. 30m/100ft

***Hedera helix* 'Angularis Aurea'** E: ◑
A decorative golden ivy whose colour
lightens a part-shady corner, though its
yellow will fade if it receives no sun. Self-
clinging. 4m/13ft

***Hydrangea anomala petiolaris* (Climbing
hydrangea)** ◑ ●
Although this plant climbs with aerial
roots, give it support when young. White
flowers in lacy corymbs in summer. Moist,
leafy soil. 6m/20ft

***Parthenocissus henryana* ◑
●**
A beautiful self-clinging
climber with bronze-green
pale-veined leaves in
summer that turn to
crimson velvet in autumn.
9m/30ft

***Schizophragma integrifolium* ◑**
The large flower-heads of this self-clinging climber are
borne in summer and surrounded by showy white
bracts. Like the climbing hydrangea, it can be slow to
get going and will benefit from help and a humus-rich
soil. 12m/39ft

Pergolas and Arbours

Pergolas originated in Italy where they were used as a method of growing vines until it became apparent how decoratively they could support all manner of climbing plants. Usually made from stone, brick or timber piers topped by horizontal cross-beams, they make cool, airy pathways, partly shaded in summer by their canopy of abundant foliage and flowers. At one extreme they can be installed in prosaic surroundings connecting, for example, a garage with a house door; or, shown at their most enchanting, they can form a canopy to a small bridge across water, the whole graceful structure reflected in the stream.

Bowers or arbours are the simplest to make of these ornamental features, just summerhouses formed from climbing plants trained to cover and weep over a structure of iron or timber. The most inviting spot to build an arbour is in the sunshiny nook made between two walls, so long as it faces an engaging view.

CLIMBERS FOR PERGOLAS AND ARBOURS

Suitable plants are to be found in the following list. Always relate their habit to the size of the structure they must festoon.

Clematis in variety p.224
Hedera (ivy) in variety
Humulus lupulus 'Aureus' p.62
Jasminum officinale p.148
Lonicera (honeysuckle) in variety p.47
Solanum crispum 'Glasnevin' p.229
Vitis 'Brant'
Vitis coignetiae p.230
Vitis vinifera purpurea p.230
Wisteria sinensis p.230
Wisteria floribunda p.230

Climbing roses need choosing with care since they need to be flexible. Also most are too tall for the verticals and will flower out of sight at the top but the following are suitable.

R. 'Albertine'
R. 'Bleu Magenta'
R. 'Blush Noisette'
R. 'New Dawn'

Rosa **'Albertine'**
An old favourite and a robust rambler which produces a mass of double salmon-pink flowers in summer. Better on a pergola than a wall as it is liable to mildew in a dry position. 5m/15ft

***Rosa* 'Bleu Magenta'**
A sumptuously dark rambling rose with small very
double flowers which look wonderful hanging in
garlands along a pergola in high summer. 4.5m/15ft

***Rosa* 'Blush Noisette'**
A very pretty climbing noisette for a sheltered position.
It produces fairly continuous flowers in summer and as
it is short-growing, is ideal for a small arbour. 2.1m/7ft

Climbers and their Hosts

One of the most elegant ways of cultivating climbing plants is to grow them in layers. A robust, mature, stiff host plant supports a more fragile, lanky climbing plant, and in a small garden it is an ideal way of introducing diversity, for two or even three plants are grown over the same space.

Pairing the 'host' plant and its 'guest' is a matter partly of common sense, partly of knowing how each grows, and partly of aesthetic taste. Obviously both plants should enjoy the same aspect and soil. Equally obvious is the fact that the host plant should be stout and mature enough to resist being smothered by the climber enveloping it. Pair those plants which flower at different seasons and you enjoy a double display in the same area.

Possible host plants include cotoneasters, berberis, evergreens with very small leaves like yew or cypress, pyracantha, and viburnum. Trees can also be suitable, such as old, fruitless apple or pear trees which can make excellent hosts. So do many small trees whose outer branches dip low enough to the ground, so that the climber (planted at this outer perimeter, well out of range of the tree's greedy roots) can be trained to grow up this framework.

Rosa 'Paul's Himalayan Musk' festoons an old apple tree. Rambler roses like this flower only once in summer but the blooms can be so abundant that they completely cover the host.

This *Clematis montana* 'Grandiflora' looks very pretty over *Ceanothus* 'Blue Mound' but it will have to be removed. Always take care that a climber doesn't throttle its host. The clematis here will kill this ceanothus if it is allowed to remain over its branches.

Climbing roses can be both hosts and guests. An old
pear tree supports *Rosa filipes* 'Kiftsgate', as a guest. This
huge rambler rose grows so large it is almost
uncontrollable so it can only be grown in the right
circumstances.

This climbing rose
provides the supporting
framework for a clematis.
Climbing roses make a
stiffer framework than
rambling roses.

Vitis coignetiae, which is a truly lusty climber, drapes itself
over a large pine, a brilliant combination as the autumn
tints of the vine leaves glow against the blue pine
needles. However, a rampant climber like this might
damage the tree.

Trees

A small tree is a substantial asset in all but the tiniest gardens, bestowing shade near a house and effecting a change of height which is always essential to engage interest. And if it can be planted to the side of the garden and allowed to overhang slightly one of the walls or fences, it will also help to dispel the feeling of claustrophobia sometimes induced by small enclosures.

Since it will be a dominant plant, the tree deserves to be chosen with care. Perhaps spectacular flowers at one season are the most important feature, or a beautifully marked bark which will look handsome throughout the year. A graceful evergreen tree may be preferable whose leaves help to keep the garden clothed at all seasons. Or instead will a tree be needed to bear edible fruit?

In larger gardens there is room for more choice about the kinds of trees and their positions. They don't have to be planted on their own as specimens. It is worth bearing in mind that small trees are often worthwhile in the shrub border where they break the bushy monotony and give extra height. Even in the large mixed or herbaceous border, they may have a part to play. One on its own can be the dominant plant around which the rest of the border is assembled. Or a number of the same species planted at even intervals will give formal regularity to the border. For this purpose the fastigiate conifers on page 246 are the most useful.

Amelanchier canadensis
LH
Dense deciduous tree with white flowers in spring, richly colouring leaves in autumn. Sometimes a shrubby habit. 6 × 3m/ 20 × 10ft

Acer pseudoplatanus
'Brilliantissimum'
Slow-growing mop-head. New foliage in spring is soft salmon pink, turning to yellow-green. 6 × 7m/20 × 23ft

Magnolia × loebneri 'Leonard Messel'
A beautiful lime-tolerant hybrid with delicate flowers on
bare branches before the pale green leaves develop.
8 × 6m/26 × 20ft

Magnolia salicifolia LH
Most beautiful mass of
12cm/5in pure white
scented flowers in spring
on the leafless branches.
Willow-like leaves. Conical
habit. 10 × 5m/33 × 16ft

There is a further
selection of trees in
other sections:
Plants for Heavy Clay
  Soils pp. 16–19
Plants for Alkaline
  Soils pp. 26–9
Plants for Lime-free or
  Acid Soils pp.36–9
Gold and Green
  pp.64–7
Grey and Silver
  pp.72–3

Magnolia × soulangeana LH: ○
The most popular and adaptable of the magnolias with
spectacular, goblet-shaped flowers in spring before the
leaves open. It is tolerant of clay soils and atmospheric
pollution. There are a number of fine clones, including

'Alba' (above left). 'Lennei' (above right), 'Rustica
Rubra' (the outside is rosy-crimson) and 'Brozzoni'
with especially large white flowers bearing a purple
stain at the base. The tree is usually rather shrubby
and wide-spreading. 6m/20ft H and W

Malus floribunda
The low, bushy, very
broad-headed Japanese
crab-apple tree bearing
masses of small flowers
which are rosy-red in bud
and pink fading to white
when open. Small red and
yellow fruits in autumn.
5 × 6m/16 × 20ft

Malus × moerlandsii 'Profusion'
Crab apple with wine-red flowers in late spring and
purple-red 2.5cm/1in fruit in autumn. Purplish juvenile
foliage, ageing to bronze-green. 6 × 4m/20 × 13ft

***Prunus cerasifera* 'Pissardii'**
Soft pink flowers in very early spring, new foliage ruby
red, turning heavy purple later in year. 6m/20ft H and
W but sometimes clipped to a mop-head. *Prunus ×
blireana* is similar, but flowers later, bronzed leaf.
10m/33ft H and W

***Prunus* 'Amanogawa'**
Very narrow columnar habit, useful for limited spaces.
Casts little shade. Semi-double, pale pink flowers in
spring. 10 × 4m/33 × 13ft

***Prunus* 'Pink Shell'**
A beautiful member of a family which are all excellent
subjects for limy soil. It has spreading branches and
semi-double flowers opening in spring. The leaves
usually colour red and orange in autumn.
9 × 8m/30 × 26ft

239

Cornus florida rubra ○
Bushy, wide-spreading tree with beautiful rosy-pink
bracts surrounding its flowers in early summer. But
performs well only in areas with reliably warm summers.
5 × 7m/16 × 23ft

Eucryphia* × *nymansensis E
Glorious late-summer flowering tree which needs its
roots shaded and some protection from cold winds. For
moist, well-drained soils. It has an erect habit and
tolerates a degree of alkalinity in the soil.
15 × 4m/49 × 13ft

Halesia monticola (Snowdrop tree)
This spreading or conical tree, a North American native,
is happier on lime-free soils. White bells hang from the
underside of branches in late spring. 8 × 10m/26 × 33ft

CONSIDER ALSO:
Prunus subhirtella
'Autumnalis', a most
valuable tree near a
house for its winter
beauty. Its delicate
white (or palest pink in
the form 'Rosea') bell-
shaped flowers open in
small, intermittent
flushes from late
autumn throughout
the winter, the
remainder blooming in
spring. Spreading,
densely-twigged
crown. 8m/26ft H and
W

Genista aetnensis ○
A shrub with a tree-like habit. Support initially with a
stake. Its green stems are almost leafless so it casts
virtually no shade and is ideal for the mixed and
herbaceous border. Gold flowers in summer. 5m/16ft H
and W

Koelreuteria paniculata ○
A domed, picturesque tree with branching panicles up
to 45cm/1¹/₂ft long of golden flowers in late summer.
Its long, dark green pinnate leaves open as deep red
in late spring and turn yellow in autumn. Full sun is
preferable. 10m/33ft H and W

Cornus alternifolia subsp. **'Argentea'**
The variegated pagoda dogwood, a shrubby tree, needs
room for the display of its tiered pattern of branches
which grow like stacked plates. Silver variegated leaves.
3 × 2.1m/10 × 7ft

Acer griseum **(Paperbark maple)** ○
A most desirable tree with a peeling rufous bark and
trifoliate leaves that turn red and gold in autumn.
8 × 6m/26 × 20ft

Eucalyptus pauciflora subsp. ***niphophila*** E: ○
Rather gaunt, reasonably hardy, slow-growing,
evergreen tree with wonderfully patterned green, grey
and cream bark which should not be obscured by
neighbouring plants. Casts very little shade.
10 × 8m/33 × 26ft

Prunus serrula
A vigorous tree with a
polished mahogany-red
bark which is handsome at
all times of the year.
Dullish green leaves which
tend to hide the mass of
very small white flowers in
late spring. 8m/26ft H and
W

***Prunus pendula* 'Pendula Rosea'**
Forms an extraordinary, spreading hummock whose
pendulous branches are fascinating even in winter
bareness. Flowers in spring and needs a great deal of
lateral space. 5 × 7m/16 × 23ft

***Cotoneaster frigidus* 'Cornubia'** semi-E
Useful for its persistent red berries in autumn onwards, semi-evergreen leaf, vigour and tolerance of difficult sites, but wide-spreading and ultimately up to 7m/23ft H and W

***Arbutus unedo* (Killarney strawberry tree)** E
Darkish-red bark, dark evergreen leaves, and highly ornamental strawberry-like fruits in late autumn at the same time as the white flower-bells open. The form 'Rubra' has pinkish flowers. (The fruit is edible but unpalatable.) 5m/16ft H and W

***Malus* 'Evereste'**
Pink-white flowers mass this dwarf crab apple in spring followed by scarlet fruit in autumn. 3.5 x 2.4m/13 x 8ft. There are a number of other ornamental hybrid apples including the excellent 'Red Sentinel' whose glossy red fruits persist for months on the tree.

Sorbus commixta (Japanese Rowan)
A vigorous rowan with glossy green leaves that turn purple and scarlet in autumn. The white flowers of spring are followed by clusters of brilliant orange-red berries. 10 x 5m/33 x 16ft

Sorbus hupehensis
This rowan has long silvery glaucous leaflets, orange-red in autumn. Its white yellow-centred flowers in spring are succeeded by green berries that turn white or blush pink. 13 × 8m/43 × 26ft

Sorbus vilmorinii
A very pretty rowan though it is sometimes a weak grower. Its deeply divided leaves are a dark grey-green, reddening in late autumn. White spring flowers are followed by fruits that are notable for their charming variation in colour, starting dark rose-red, and developing in stages through pink to blush white. 4 × 5m/ 13 × 16ft

Sorbus sargentiana
A magnificent broad-headed rowan which makes one of the great autumn displays. Its green leaflets turn rich scarlet and gold in autumn. Its flat white inflorescences in spring are followed by large dazzling clusters of red berries. 6m/20ft H and W

SLIM CONIFERS AND EVERGREEN TREES

These can be planted as specimen trees or used to make a narrow focal point (or series of focal points) in beds and borders.

CONSIDER ALSO:
Juniperus virginiana 'Skyrocket'
Chamaecyparis lawsoniana 'Kilmacurragh'

***Juniperus chinensis* 'Aurea'** E: ○
A slow-growing and very slim column of golden-foliage which looks particularly handsome forming a spire in a border as here. 8 × 1.2m/26 × 4ft

***Taxus baccata* 'Fastigiata' (Irish Yew)** E
This slender form of yew is slow, makes a broad column eventually.
10 × 3m/33 × 10ft

***Juniperus communis* 'Hibernica'** E
This forms a very narrow column of blue-grey foliage and is an excellent accent subject. Its growth is slow but as it ages, it may need tying in to keep it erect.
4m × 45cm/13 × 1½ft

***Chamaecyparis lawsoniana* 'Columnaris'** E: ○
A pencil slim conifer with blue-grey spice-scented foliage. It broadens slightly with age but will take a little clipping. 9 × 1.2m/30 × 4ft

CONSIDER ALSO:
Pinus radiata p.221

Gingko biloba

Marvellous tree which is one of the main choices for a large garden. A deciduous conifer which is the only survivor of an important family of trees in existence 160 million years ago. Held sacred in the East and found planted by Buddhist temples. Exquisite ribbed foliage, yellowing in autumn on a columnar tree when young, which broadens with age. Slow growth. 25 × 7m/80 × 23ft

Cedrus libani subsp. *atlantica* 'Glauca' (Blue Atlas cedar) ○

This magnificent vigorous tree needs plenty of space in a large garden. It bears barrel-shaped cones of 7.5cm/3in. Its silvery-blue foliage, especially brilliant in spring, size and elegant conical shape make it outstanding. 16 × 9m/ 52 × 30ft

Pinus wallichiana (syns. *excelsa, griffithii*) E

Fine, fast-growing and fairly adaptable pine, though not for shallow chalk, with blue-grey-green needles, 20cm/8in long, and curving cones which can be yet longer. Soft, almost feathery appearance. 15 × 10m/ 50 × 33ft

Picea breweriana E

Another very beautiful conifer called 'Brewer's Weeping Spruce', which is hung with deep green curtains of 60cm/2ft long branchlets. Slow growing. 10 × 7m/33 × 23ft

Index

Acknowledgements

Many of the photographs were taken in the author's garden. The publishers would also like to thank the many people and organizations whose gardens have appeared in this book, including the following: Barnsley House, Barnsley, Cirencester; Burford House, Tenbury Wells; Chilcombe House, Chilcombe, Dorset; Dr A. and Dr. L. Cox, Woodpeckers, Marlcliff, Bidford-on-Avon; Denmans, Denmans Lane, Fontwell; Eastgrove Cottage Garden Nursery, Sankyns Green, Shrawley, Worcester; Richard Edwards, Well Cottage, Blakemere; Frampton Manor, Frampton; The Hon Mrs Peter Healing, The Priory, Kemerton; Lance Hattatt, Arrow Cottage, Ledgemoor, Weobley; Hergest Croft, Kington; Hodges Barn, Shipton Moyne; Kim Hurst, The Cottage Herbery, Boraston, Tenbury Wells; Kiftsgate Court, near Chipping Campden; Oxford Botanic Gardens; Mrs Richard Paice, Bourton House Garden, Bourton-on-the-Hill, Moreton-in-Marsh; The Picton Garden, Colwall; Anthony Poulton, 21 Swinton Lane, Worcester; Powis Castle (National Trust); Tony Ridler, 7 St Peters Terrace, Cockett, Swansea; Royal Botanic Gardens, Kew; RHS Garden, Wisley; Paul and Betty Smith, The Old Chapel, Ludlow; Stone House Cottage, Kidderminster; Raymond Treasure, Stockton Bury Gardens, Kimbolton; The Weir, Swainshill, Hereford (National Trust); Wakehurst Place (National Trust); Whitfield, Wormbridge.

The photograph on the front cover shows part of Rosemary Verey's garden at Barnsley House, Gloucestershire, in spring.

256